A CONCISE G
ORCHESTRA(

1700 TO THE PRESENT DAY

MB20700

BY DAVID FLIGG

BILL'S MUSIC SHELF

Visit us on the Web at www.melbay.com or www.billsmusicshelf.com

David Fligg is Principal Lecturer in Classical Music, at Leeds College of Music, England. His research interests and teaching specialisms include contemporary classical composition, and music history and analysis. As a writer, he has contributed to a number of journals, and has written program and CD liner notes for many of the world's leading orchestras and musicians. He is currently involved in various higher education music related consultancies, as well as guest lecturing and conducting on a freelance basis. A graduate of the University of Leeds, from where he also holds a Doctorate, he gained his M.Mus. from London University's Royal Holloway College, and is a Fellow of the Higher Education Academy.

In memory of Alma Peters

To Ian,

Do not judge me too
harshly on the contents of
this book!

All good wishes,

Dad

Leeds, December 2010

Contents

ILLUSTRATIONS

FOREWORD

This book, intended for the general public, music students, and enthusiasts of all ages, explores the history of orchestral music, from its origins up to the present day. Dr. David Fligg, an academic and composer deeply involved in music education for many years, has written a fascinating guide to a complex subject, illuminating the development of orchestral composition over the course of history with profound insight and clarity. I would like to express my gratitude to William Bay and all his staff at Mel Bay Publications Inc. for making this book possible, and to my wife, Elizabeth, for her invaluable editorial assistance during the preparation of this work.

Graham Wade
General Editor – *ALL ABOUT MUSIC SERIES*

ACKNOWLEDGEMENTS

I would like to thank those who supported me in the writing of this book. Firstly, my thanks to Graham and Beth Wade for their helpful editorial guidance, mentoring and valued friendship. To friends and family, I say thanks for allowing me to impose chunks of text on you, and for spotting my typos. Thanks to Peter Whitfield and Randall Whittaker for the many hours we've spent discussing repertoire, listening to music, debating and pouring over scores. Thanks to my students who have been on the receiving-end of my ideas within the book. Always not least, thanks to Adrian for his patience and encouragement, and for having had to live with this book and its author.

David Fligg, PhD, M.Mus, BA(Hons), FHEA
Leeds, England, 2008

INTRODUCTION

Every evening in concert halls around the world, audiences settle down to listen to orchestras, professional and amateur alike, perform repertoire by the great composers. It would be an interesting exercise to ascertain just how many performances of, say, Beethoven's *Eroica Symphony*, Tchaikovsky's *First Piano Concerto*, or the Bach *Brandenburg Concertos* – to name but a few well-known works – are being performed or broadcast at any one time. These composers would be astounded by such popularity which, with the recent information technology and communications revolution, increases unabated.

It was not always thus, for three main reasons. Firstly, the Beethoven and Tchaikovsky works cited above did not start life in a blaze of adoration and popularity. Secondly, Bach saw himself primarily as an artisan; he was not writing for posterity. Thirdly, until the end of the eighteenth century, there was little concept of the public concert. Eventually, music-making ceased to be the preserve of well-heeled aristocrats, as the new middle classes used their money to pay to listen to music, much of it newly composed. So, whereas Bach's music was performed in his lifetime almost exclusively in those places where he lived, Beethoven's music was performed, during his lifetime, abroad, including the United States.

We all too often take for granted the fact that well-known and much loved repertoire, such as the pieces referred to above, represent great music – however we might define the word 'great'. The aim of the following chapters is to present a guide as to why such music has stood the test of time, and to help the listener identify the innovative quality of the music, thereby capturing some of its genius.

The readership for this book will be a broad one. It is not intended for specialist musicians, but rather for music-lovers, concertgoers, school-age students hoping to study music at a higher level, and undergraduate music students. All of the music mentioned is available on recordings, though such accessibility is not always an indicator of popularity or worth.

Consequently, this book largely concentrates, though not exclusively, on music which appears, or has appeared, in live performance on the international concert platform. Inevitably, some composers are more popular in some parts of the world, than in others. Where composers have an almost exclusively national, rather than international, reputation, they have generally not been mentioned.

The following guidelines will assist the reader. This book does not deal directly with biography, though biographical details are included where deemed necessary. The narrative runs more or less chronologically, though occasionally some artistic license is employed, especially where composers straddle centuries. For example, Elgar is a case in point. He lived for forty-three years in the nineteenth century, and thirty-four in the twentieth, yet composed almost all his significant music in a short period between 1899 and 1919.

There are other similar instances, but they should not cause too many tears for the reader. The early eighteenth century poses something of an interesting dilemma. Relatively little orchestral music from the eighteenth century finds its way into the regular, familiar repertoire. Moreover, the line where Baroque chamber music ends, and orchestral begins, is a somewhat vague one. Consequently, and inevitably, the Baroque is not dealt with in any great detail. Beethoven is given a chapter to himself, as few would disagree that he was seminal in the development of much that followed. It might seem that some composers receive disproportionate attention. Rachmaninov is a case in point. It should be remembered though, that in his case, though he was no great innovator, his music is amongst the most frequently performed and recorded of all time. It is difficult to determine which orchestral works written in the final part of the twentieth century and the beginning of the twenty-first will be performed by later generations. Therefore, the final section offers a summary rather than specifics.

Choral, vocal and chamber works are occasionally mentioned where such citation helps to place a composer or a set of works in context. Largely, however, choral symphonies, for instance, are not discussed at any length. Consequently, some significant composers who are mainly noted for writing vocal or chamber music are not within the scope of this book. For example, Verdi, one of the most notable of nineteenth century composers, is remembered almost exclusively for his operas. Music for string orchestra is discussed, as a large string orchestra could have fifty or more players. Other types of ensemble music, such as that for wind or percussion ensemble, or concert band, are generally not dealt with. Composers who wrote mainly for the cinema are outside the scope of this book.

Unless otherwise stated, the given dates of compositions in parentheses indicate when they were completed. Where works are universally referred to in language other than English (for example, the *Eroica Symphony*), their translated title is normally not offered. Similarly, a translation is not given where non-English titles are almost identical in both languages (for example, *Sinfonia Domestica*). Occasionally, the English is given in parentheses to a foreign title, and vice-versa, depending on which language the work is most frequently described in.

For example, Mahler's *Das Lied von der Erde* is usually always referred to as *The Song of the Earth* in English-speaking countries. However, his *Kindertotenlieder* is rarely referred to in its English translation. Opus, Köchel and other catalog numbers are generally not included, unless there is potential confusion with another work.

CHAPTER 1

—

Setting the Scene

A substantial part of this book will discuss symphonies, for the symphony has been the predominant orchestral genre since the second half of the eighteenth century. Alongside the symphony is the concerto, a somewhat older genre, and one which reflects increased dexterity on, and the development of, various instruments. The symphony, too, has been re-invented over the generations because of various circumstances, but not least due to the development of the orchestra itself. Indeed, it is a moot point as to whether orchestral music resulted in technical developments of instruments, or whether the instruments themselves had a direct influence on orchestral genres; a bit of both, one suspects. As orchestral music became increasingly complex, the structure of the music itself took on something of a change, not least in the development of what we now call sonata form. Add to this the various periods, or styles, of music, which we conveniently label, and which fall under our period of discussion. This chapter will present a brief overview of all of this.

Periods In Music

We live in a society which enjoys the exercise of pigeon holing and labelling. This is no less true in music, and the era since the beginning of the eighteenth century is split into a number of periods. The Baroque period lasted approximately from 1600 to 1750. The age of Bach, Handel, Vivaldi and their contemporaries in the first half of the eighteenth century is known as the high Baroque. Like all periods and styles, it had its own favorite musical forms, such as the suite, trio sonata and concerto grosso, and the predominance of certain instruments, notably the harpsichord.

The language here is defined by its reliance on polyphony, or counterpoint to give it its technical name, where seemingly independent melodic lines weave in and out of each other to create a harmonic whole. Figured bass, or thoroughbass as it is sometimes known, was extensively used as a shorthand way of notating harmony for the continuo part, the ubiquitous sound of the harpsichord which helped to fill in the harmonic structure of the music. It was during the Baroque period that the standard harmonic vocabulary of major and minor keys, and their hierarchy of chords, was established.

Around the middle of the eighteenth century, there emerged a transitional style between the Baroque and Classical periods, sometimes known as Rococo or Style Galant. Composers of this period include Bach's sons who, incidentally, considered their father to be something of an anachronism, and some of the earlier music of Haydn and Mozart. The later part of the eighteenth century is known as the Classical period and was chiefly, though of course not exclusively, dominated by Haydn and Mozart. The piano began to emerge as a versatile solo instrument, ultimately to replace the harpsichord. The continuo and use of figured bass eventually fell from grace, the symphony and solo concerto were firmly established, and sonata form became the chief means by which composers could create large-scale orchestral and instrumental structures.

It was also the period in which the modern orchestra, to all intents and purposes, was established.

Undoubtedly, the earlier works of Beethoven and Schubert can be described as Classical, and these composers, Beethoven in particular, are often cited as examples of a transitional style between the Classical and Romantic periods. Certainly, by 1830 it would seem that Romanticism was the order of the day. With nineteenth century Romanticism came the ascendancy of program, or descriptive, music. Running alongside this was the rise of the virtuoso performer, usually pianists and violinists and, inevitably, the music written for these people was far more technically demanding than more or less anything which had come before. Instruments began to be refined, with more key-work on woodwinds, and valves for trumpets and horns.

By the second half of the century, the piano had developed into the instrument that it is today, and orchestras in the nineteenth century became larger. Public concerts, which until the end of the eighteenth century were almost non-existent, had become within a short space of time, and certainly by the 1820s, a popular pastime for the moneyed middle classes which industrial and political revolution had defined. Political change also brought with it national consciousness and the nationalism of such composers as Dvořák, Smetana and others.

In truth, the age of Romanticism never ended. It is just that by the twentieth century, it was something of a free-for-all as far as stylistic boundaries were concerned. The twentieth century was the century of 'isms', such as expressionism, serialism, neo-classicism, impressionism, with nationalism still holding its own. It was now open season for composers to explore and use whatever language they felt was relevant. Just to offer one snapshot: around 1920, there were composers as diverse as Schoenberg, Stravinsky, Bartók, Ravel, Richard Strauss, Rachmaninov, Elgar, Janáček, Sibelius, Puccini and Vaughan Williams – to mention a mere handful – composing in widely divergent styles. Add to this the rise of jazz and popular music. The same is true today in the early years of the new millennium.

With all of the above, comes something of a health warning. Styles and periods evolve gradually and merge imperceptibly. There were those composing in an overtly Baroque style in 1750, and at the same time those experimenting in ideas which were to fuel the Classical period. In the 1830s, Berlioz was already using huge orchestras, whilst Mendelssohn was content with those of Classical proportions. Richard Strauss's *Four Last Songs* were composed in 1948, and sound as if they could have been written fifty years earlier, so rooted in the Austro-German Romantic tradition are they. Yet almost at the same time, the post-war *avant-garde* of the so-called Darmstadt School was perplexing audiences and sending young composers in completely new and audacious directions.

The Orchestra

By the end of the eighteenth century, there emerged what was basically the standard symphony orchestra. In their later works, Haydn and Mozart set a yardstick for a standardized line-up of orchestral forces. This consisted of two each of flutes, oboes, clarinets, bassoons, horns and trumpets, two timpani tuned to tonic and dominant, and a string section of two sets of violins, violas, cellos and double basses. Even so, Haydn and Mozart frequently used fewer winds than this. Whilst the size of the winds was always specified, there was more fluidity with the size of the string section, though its basic line-up of five sections never differed. Even today, the exact number of string players will differ from orchestra to orchestra. Typically, a late eighteenth century string section might consist of three desks (ie, six players) of first violins, two desks of second violins, one or two desks of violas, a desk of cellos and a double bass. Exceptions were common. For example, as early as 1753, the Dresden Orchestra had fifteen violins, four violas and three each of cellos and basses.

Haydn's orchestra at Esterháza in the 1780s had twenty-four players of which twenty were strings. The orchestra lacked clarinets, trumpets and timpani, which would have been brought in when required. By the 1820s, it seems that the first performance of Beethoven's *Ninth Symphony* had at least forty strings.

So whilst there was some standardization in orchestral lay-outs by the end of the eighteenth century, the Baroque period had no benchmark for orchestra size. A glance at the forces used in Bach's *Brandenburg Concertos* of 1721 demonstrates that Bach, like his contemporaries, would use whatever was available. There are hardly any two Baroque works with exactly the same instrumentation and, in any case, so-called Baroque orchestral music is what we might today define as chamber music, because the forces used were almost invariably modest.

As the eighteenth century progressed, standardization crept in. The woodwind section was enlarged during the Classical period to include clarinets. Timpani became less of a novelty, and more of a standard, though any additional percussion was rare until the nineteenth century. Trombones were not introduced to the symphony orchestra until Beethoven's *Fifth Symphony* in 1808, although they were used by the Classical composers in opera and church music. By the 1840s, trumpets and horns with the newly-invented valves were rapidly replacing non-chromatic instruments, thereby offering greater flexibility to composers. The tuba was invented in the 1830s, and soon found its way into the orchestra. Adolphe Sax helped to develop this instrument, though he is chiefly remembered as the inventor of the saxophone in 1840, yet its inclusion in symphonic music is still relatively rare.

Public Concerts

Running alongside the development of the orchestra, was the rise of public concerts. Until the eighteenth century, concerts took place before invited guests in the homes of the aristocracy. Religious works were performed in churches, thereby offering the poor or uneducated the only opportunity of hearing good quality, and well-performed music, though opera houses began to be established in Italy in the seventeenth century. There were isolated instances of public concerts in the seventeenth and early eighteenth centuries. But it was the Concerts Spirituels, established in Paris in 1725, and where Mozart's *Paris Symphony* was premiered, which gave other cities the impetus to gradually introduce public concerts.

For example, and perhaps most eminently, 1781 saw the establishment of concerts at Leipzig's Gewandhaus, the old cloth hall, though in fact Leipzig had established subscription concerts some forty years earlier. Public concerts were initiated in London, Vienna and Berlin in the 1770s. Haydn composed his London symphonies for Johann Salomon's public concerts in the 1790s. By the beginning of the nineteenth century, public concerts were enjoying much popularity, and concert festivals grew apace, the most famous being London's Promenade Concerts, inaugurated in 1895, which to this day, known as the BBC Proms, is the world's largest classical music festival.

Sonata Form

With the rise of extended instrumental forms and the symphony, composers devised ways in which to handle larger structures. Baroque composers would use ritornello form to create extended forms, specifically in the various Baroque concerto forms. Here, a main theme, or idea, keeps returning, but is alternated with contrasting episodes. This idea of contrast and repetition was the mainstay of the Baroque, though there was little concept of actual thematic or motivic development, which came later in the eighteenth century.

The Classical composers, with Haydn at the vanguard, found that they needed a structural base in keeping with the new musical language of the Classical period, which would allow for thematic development to carry the musical argument, underpinned by the tensions and relaxations of juxtaposing keys. Sonata form, as we now describe it, thus evolved. Its exact origins are difficult to identify, and various composers played their part in its development.

Certainly, by the 1750s, there was a form which we now recognize as having sonata form characteristics. The form is sometimes referred to as first movement form since, invariably, first movements of sonatas employed it. Even so, it should be understood that other movements in other genres, such as the symphony, overture and chamber music, also use it. Since the second half of the eighteenth century, composers have been re-inventing sonata form to suit the genres of the day and the musical spirit of the age. There is, then, no such thing as textbook sonata form and, in any case, the term itself was not coined until the nineteenth century.

Although exceptions abound, in its eighteenth century incarnation, the form has three main components: exposition, development and recapitulation. The exposition consists of the first and second subject groups, each group containing a main theme or themes. A bridge passage links the two groups, and allows the music to modulate to a closely related key for the second subject. After the second subject, there is a codetta which ends the exposition in the key of the second subject.

The exposition is often repeated and, in a first movement, it might be prefaced by a slow introduction. The development section literally develops and explores ideas first heard in the exposition. Compared with the exposition, the development is fairly short. The recapitulation comes next, and this follows the same scheme as the exposition, except that both first and second subjects are in the same key. A coda rounds things off. Occasionally, the recapitulation is repeated.

Sometimes, the main theme of the second subject is the same as the first subject, though in a different key. The first movement of Haydn's *London Symphony* is a well-known example of this. With Beethoven, the coda eventually became something of a second development. In fact, Beethoven radically expanded the form from a movement lasting, perhaps, seven or eight minutes, to one lasting almost twenty minutes in some cases. Later in the nineteenth century, Bruckner and Mahler expanded it even further in terms of duration. Sonata form is, then, a dynamic and pliable form, and is still employed today by some composers to cast their musical argument.

The Symphony and Concerto

It is difficult to pinpoint exactly when the symphony made its debut on the orchestral scene. In truth, genres are not invented overnight, and the origins of the symphony as a multi-sectioned piece of orchestral music can be found in the Baroque Italian overture, with its three contrasting sections. Haydn is often attributed with being the Father of the Symphony, as he is frequently described. But, in fact, the form predates him, and Giovanni Sammartini (c.1701–1775) was composing symphonies in the 1730s, more than twenty years before Haydn. Despite these early examples, the four-movement symphony did not emerge until the 1740s and 1750s. Johann Stamitz (1717–1757), and his sons Karl (1745–1801) and Anton (1754–1809) were part of what is known as the Mannheim School, whose excellent and famous orchestra certainly played its part in the development of the symphony. This orchestra was the ideal vehicle with which to carry the new genre. For sheer innovation, though, it was

Haydn who took the symphony to new heights and, along with Mozart, profoundly influenced the greatest of the symphonists, Beethoven.

The typical late eighteenth century symphony consisted of four movements, with at least the first movement in sonata form. This movement was usually fast, followed by a slow movement in sonata, rondo or variation form. There followed a minuet with a contrasting middle, or trio, section. The work finished with a lively finale, normally in sonata or rondo form. Of course, there were exceptions to this scheme, and from Beethoven onwards, the symphony took on various shapes and sizes. Even today, it is a form employed by some contemporary composers, whether it be multi-movement or single movement, purely instrumental or vocal, programmatic or abstract.

The concerto is older than the symphony and was used during the Baroque period, from the late seventeenth century, in two main guises. One was the solo concerto, in scope not unlike the solo concertos of the Classical and Romantic periods. Here, one, or occasionally two or more solo instruments, were contrasted against a small orchestra of strings. The most well-known Baroque examples are those by Bach, Handel and Vivaldi. The other was the concerto grosso. In this, a small group of soloists, usually strings, known as the *concertino*, was contrasted against a larger body of strings, referred to as the *ripieno*. Arcangelo Corelli (1753–1713) was the great pioneer of concerti grossi.

A little later, and most famously, Bach brought the genre to exceptional sophistication in his *Brandenburg Concertos* of 1721, as did Handel with his many examples. Similar to the solo concerto, the concerto grosso invariably had three movements, and this three movement structure for concertos has remained the norm. Like the symphony, the concerto has been adapted and redefined since the eighteenth century. For example, the twentieth century saw the emergence of the concerto for orchestra, usually intended as a virtuoso display piece for orchestra, inhabiting a territory somewhere between concerto and symphony. There are notable examples of these by Bartók, Hindemith, Lutosławski and Tippett.

The twentieth century also saw the revival, after more than a century and a half, of the concerto grosso, as composers took on the mantle of neo-classicism. Examples of these include Stravinsky's *Dumbarton Oaks Concerto*, the two concerti grossi by Ernest Bloch, and Tippett's *Concerto for Double String Orchestra*, a concerto grosso in all but name.

CHAPTER 2

—

The Eighteenth Century

Bach, Handel and Vivaldi

The music of Bach, Handel and Vivaldi forms the backbone of the repertoire of the first half of the eighteenth century. This is not to say that there were no other notable composers; Corelli's concerti grossi have already been cited. Significant composers such as Jean Philippe Rameau (1683–1764), François Couperin (1668–1733), Domenico Scarlatti (1685–1757), and Georg Philipp Telemann (1681–1767), the composer of more than six hundred concertos, made their mark on the period. For orchestral music, though, attention rests on Johann Sebastian Bach (1685–1750), George Frideric Handel (1685–1759), and Antonio Vivaldi (c.1676–1741). Because there was no such concept of a standard-sized orchestra during the Baroque, it is sometimes difficult to differentiate between true orchestral music, and chamber music. Even so, it is generally accepted that the Baroque concerto and orchestral suites fit into the category of orchestral music.

The towering genius of the High Baroque was J. S. Bach, in whom we witness one of the great figures in the history of western art. A comparison with his exact, and great, contemporary, Handel, is inevitable. Both came from middle-class North German Protestant backgrounds. Here the similarities end. While Handel was a cosmopolitan who traveled widely, Bach, on the other hand, preferred to stay in his native region. Handel composed for a wide audience, at a time when public concerts were all but unheard of. He invested fortunes in his ventures, especially operatic ones. Bach wrote for small occasions and was happy to earn a living to support a large family, whereas Handel never married.

In his day, Antonio Vivaldi, born in Venice, Italy, became known as the Red-Headed Priest, on account of his shock of red hair, and as he was actually an ordained priest. However, it was as a musician that he made his living. For almost forty years, until just prior to his death, he taught at the Music Seminary of the Ospizio della Pietà in Venice. This convent had a strong musical tradition, and many of his compositions were written initially for the girls there.

His famously celebrated works, amongst the most frequently performed music of the period, are the four concertos which comprise *The Four Seasons* – program music which is inspired by an extra-musical idea. Although we tend to think of program music as being primarily a nineteenth century innovation, it can, in fact, be traced back to the middle ages.

However, Vivaldi was one of the first composers to write a substantial number of instrumental compositions which are based on images of nature. Apart from *The Four Seasons* concertos, *La Notte (Night)*, *La Tempesta di Mare (The Storm at Sea)*, *Il Gardellino (The Goldfinch)* and *Concerto alla Rustica*, belong to the same tradition. And from here, we can trace the path towards Beethoven's *Pastoral Symphony* and beyond, via Haydn's *Le Matin, Le Midi,* and *Le Soir* symphonies.

We do not know how many concertos Vivaldi composed, as some have been lost, and some are incomplete. The extant concertos number around four hundred and ninety-four, and there could have been as many as five hundred and thirty. Of these, three hundred and twenty-nine are concertos for one soloist and orchestra, like *The Four Seasons*. The rest encompass double concertos and other types of Baroque concerto form.

With such a plethora of works in one genre, it should come as no surprise that the concertos are not of a consistently high quality, which has led to the oft-quoted remark that Vivaldi composed not four hundred and ninety-four concertos, but one concerto four hundred and ninety-four times! Nonetheless, Bach was impressed enough by them to make keyboard arrangements from some of them, and *The Four Seasons* in particular contain some of Vivaldi's best music.

The Four Seasons comprise: *Concerto in E, Spring*; *Concerto in G minor, Summer*; *Concerto in F, Autumn*; *Concerto in F minor, Winter*. They are the first of twelve concertos grouped together as *Opus 8*, published in Amsterdam in 1730, and dedicated to Count Morzin, whose family were later to employ Haydn. The works are scored for solo violin, strings and harpsichord continuo, though they are occasionally adapted as flute concertos. Each concerto is prefaced by a poem, probably by Vivaldi himself.

Bach was thirty-three years old when, in 1717, he relinquished his post as organist and court musician at Weimar, and entered service for Prince Leopold of Anhalt-Cöthen. Bach's first large-scale work there was composing the *Brandenburg Concertos* (1721). They are, quite simply, amongst the finest instrumental works ever written, diverse in character and brimming with invention. The concertos were commissioned by Prince Christian Ludwig, Margrave of the Prussian province of Brandenburg.

Although these works came together as a result of this commission, it is almost certain that they were in fact for the court orchestra at Cöthen. Judging from the highly intricate and virtuosic orchestral writing, this orchestra must have been an exceptionally fine one. It is doubtful whether the Margrave of Brandenburg ever had these concertos played, and they were only rescued by chance from his library after his death.

Each of the six concertos is written for a different group of instrumentalists. The *Third* and *Sixth* resemble the Baroque concerto grosso, whereas the other concertos use groups of instruments in a more soloistic manner, and because of this amalgam of styles, these works are not true examples of concerti grossi. Indeed, the diverse selection and combination of instruments has inevitably resulted in much speculation about Bach's true intentions with regard to his instrumental forces.

Moreover, some of the instrumentation deliberately combines old and new. For example, in the *Sixth Concerto*, the almost archaic use of viols (viola da gamba) is contrasted with the more modern violas. And in the *Fifth Concerto*, the harpsichord is used both in the traditional Baroque manner of continuo, as well as a solo-concerto instrument.

For modern performances of any eighteenth century music, especially from the Baroque period, there are problems, and these might be concerned with the instruments themselves, authenticity of the score or its edition, or problems of notation and performance. Unless an ensemble specializes in authentically recreating a Baroque sound, complete with original or replica eighteenth century instruments and instrumental technique, then compromise – and common sense – have to be relied upon, even though we know far more about how to perform Baroque music than we did before, say, 1960. In the *Brandenburgs*, for example, modern treble recorders or flutes usually have to replace Bach's 'fifara' in the *Fourth Concerto* (and we are not entirely sure what exactly he meant by 'fifara').

In the *Second Concerto*, the precariously high trumpet part is now sometimes played on a modern E flat (piccolo) clarinet, if a Baroque trumpet is not available. Other issues concern tempo and performance indications. It was not until the second half of the eighteenth century that composers became more specific about such details, and we therefore often have to make a calculated guess at the speed of much Baroque music. Usually, this is fairly obvious for anyone with a fair degree of sensitivity of style and genre, though sometimes a number of vastly varying speeds could suit the same piece.

The first movement of the *Third Brandenburg Concerto* typifies this problem. More often than not performed in a moderate four beats per bar, it seems more likely that Bach intended a faster, two beats per bar, tempo – yet both tempi can be made to sound musically satisfying. Similarly, those performance indications relating to volume of sound (dynamics), or whether notes should be played smoothly (legato) or detached (staccato) – i.e. articulation – is largely absent from much Baroque music.

In addition to the *Brandenburgs*, Bach completed eleven solo concertos, plus six which are arrangements of his own, or Vivaldi's, concertos, though orchestral music occupies a relatively small part of Bach's output. The *Violin Concertos in A minor* and *E minor*, the *Concerto for Two Violins in D minor*, and the *Harpsichord Concerto in D Minor*, are particularly popular, and are equal to the *Brandenburgs* in terms of invention and craftsmanship. There are also four *Orchestral Suites*; Bach gave them the title of *Overtures*. The *Third* and *Fourth* include trumpets and timpani in their line-ups, with the *Third Suite* containing the famous *Air on the G String*, as it is commonly known nowadays. The *Second Suite in B minor*, has as its finale the equally well-known *Badinerie* for flute and strings.

George Frideric Handel was more prolific at writing orchestral music than was Bach. There are 18 concerti grossi, and at least twenty- six solo concertos for various combinations. Whilst his contribution to the solo concerto is perhaps not as significant as either Bach's or Vivaldi's, his major contribution to the concerto grosso includes the twelve *Opus 6* set (1739), worthy to stand alongside the best of Bach and Vivaldi.

There are also short orchestral works which have become popular, all of them extracts from oratorios and operas. The most well-known is perhaps *The Arrival of the Queen of Sheba* from *Solomon* (1749), where two solo oboes, trumpet-like, conjure up the pomp and ceremony which must have accompanied the Queen's visit to Solomon's Jerusalem.

By far the best loved of Handel's orchestral music is the *Water Music* and *Music for the Royal Fireworks* (1749). The *Water Music* was composed for a ceremonial River Thames cruise for King George I, Handel's patron, which took place in July 1717. By eighteenth century standards, this was orchestral music on a huge scale, fit for a royal occasion, which required an orchestra of over fifty musicians on its own barge.

Because it was intended for *al fresco* performance, there is heavy reliance on wind instruments, as their sound carries outside far better than strings. A series of dance movements follows an introductory overture, though the music was later arranged into three suites, and these are the versions most often played today. The *Fireworks Music* is a suite composed to celebrate the Peace of Aix-la-Chapelle, and first performed in London's Green Park in April 1749. Whilst this music is often played in various arrangements made over the years, the original scoring was for wind instruments, and over fifty of these were employed for the first performance, including twenty-four oboes, twelve bassoons, nine trumpets and nine horns, plus three pairs of timpani – scoring ideally suited for outdoors and a noisy firework display. The rehearsal at Vauxhall earlier in the day attracted a crowd of an estimated twelve thousand. At the event itself, a salvo of ordnance led to the loss of life of a soldier, and the fireworks, which at first refused to ignite, accidentally set fire to part of the elaborate scenery.

Like Vivaldi, there is a directness and extrovertness of musical language with Handel, resulting in music which has become popular and memorable. Whilst this is plain to hear in such an astonishing masterpiece as *Messiah* – and who does not know at least a couple of items from this wonderful work? – it is also evident in the orchestral music. This is why the *Water* and *Fireworks* music, along with Bach's *Brandenburgs* and Vivaldi's *The Four Seasons*, are the most often performed and recorded works of the eighteenth century.

Haydn

Joseph Haydn (1732–1809) arrived on the scene at a crucial time in the development of European music. He was writing in that critical period between the Baroque and Classical, when styles and genres changed dramatically, and he was still composing symphonies after Mozart had ceased to do so, and merely months before Beethoven embarked on his own symphonic career. As previously explained, he did not invent the symphony, it having been around for some years before he ventured into that region. So, although his well-used sobriquet of Father of the Symphony is not quite accurate, nor is it a total misnomer. Whilst others pump-primed the genre, it was Haydn who transformed it from a mere diversion, music to accompany a patron's dinner party, into music which engaged the listener at public concerts.

Haydn's symphonies span some forty years. Many have nicknames, and as nicknamed compositions are generally easier for audiences to remember than mere numbers, several have become Haydn's most well-known works. Little of his other orchestral work is regularly performed, perhaps with the exception of one or two concertos, including the much-loved *Trumpet Concerto*.

There are one hundred and four catalogued symphonies by Haydn. We owe the current numbering and cataloging to the Breitkopf and Härtel Complete Edition, published early in the twentieth century. Haydn's own so-called draft catalog includes two additional early symphonies, plus another now lost. It should be noted, though, that Breitkopf's numbering contains some minor inaccuracies, and does not always reflect chronology. Despite subsequent research, Breitkopf's numbering is universally employed.

The sheer volume of symphonies prevents detailed discussion. But it is worthwhile to pause a moment and observe even in his early works, the type of experimentation which produced some of the most daringly original music of the eighteenth century. Whilst Haydn was, for a time, employed by Count Morzin, the symphonies he composed during that period are not as frequently performed as later ones. In 1761, Haydn obtained a new position, employed by Prince Anton Esterházy, first at the estate at Eisenstadt, and later at Esterháza.

His first symphonies for the Prince, written in 1761, are now Haydn's earliest of the frequently performed symphonies: *No. 6 in D, Le Matin*; *No. 7 in C, Le Midi*; *No. 8 in G, Le Soir*. Their fanciful titles were included on contemporary manuscripts. In this period, where musical style was transitioning from Baroque to Classical, it should not surprise us to find the use of *concertino* and *ripieno* divisions, as used in the Baroque concerto grosso, and this shows Haydn's indebtedness to the past.

Close examination of this music demonstrates Haydn the experimenter at work. For example, in *Le Matin* are three interesting orchestral effects: a cycle of *forte-piano* sequences at the end of the exposition, rare for the 1760s; effective use of pizzicato strings supporting the winds during the development; the inclusion, again quite a novelty for its time, of orchestral crescendo. The work's opening is generally thought to represent a sunrise, an idea Haydn was later to use in the oratorios *The Creation* and *The Seasons*. Later in the symphony, in the minuet's trio section, is a double-bass solo, reminding us of Haydn's acute ear for orchestral effects. There are corresponding solos in *Le Midi* and *Le Soir*, and in his day, they would have been performed on the now obsolete violone. In *Le Midi*, the concertino is extended to include oboes and bassoons, in addition to the usual strings. Haydn's avoidance of flutes in the first movement anticipates his withholding of instruments for dramatic effect in his later works.

In *Le Soir*, the first movement sounds almost like a finale, cast in 3/8 meter – unusual for a first movement – being largely mono-thematic, and opening quietly. When the finale does arrive, Haydn gives it the nickname of *La Tempesta*, a title not uncommon during the period, and a forerunner of the *Sturm und Drang* (Storm and Stress) style later in the century. As in *The Seasons* some forty years later, the flute depicts lightning. In fact, this movement is a true piece of program music, bringing to mind that famous portrayal of the elements in Vivaldi's *Four Seasons*, works which Haydn knew. Music rich in originality and ideas, and varied in language, these early symphonies set Haydn's agenda for the next forty years.

Haydn's daringness can be demonstrated by various means. He juxtaposed keys in ways which were, certainly in the 1760s and 1770s, unconventional. Quirkily, he would modulate to keys which were not closely related. There is experimentation with orchestral balance and sound, and with greater emphasis than hitherto on contrasts between loud and soft. Haydn is also known for his musical humor, some of which is obvious to any listener, as in the unexpected loud chord in the slow movement of his *Symphony No. 94, Surprise*, or the departing musicians in *Symphony No. 45, Farewell*. Other examples of musical wit are subtler, the humor of musical language, appreciated more by professional musicians.

Shortly after the completion of the symphonies discussed above, Prince Anton died, and was succeeded by Prince Nicolaus whom Haydn served until the Prince's death in 1790. Haydn's tenure under the Esterházy family was immensely fruitful, and he was well cared for and respected. By the time of Prince Nicolaus's death, Haydn was famous throughout Europe and, on this fame, was able to spend the last few years of productivity as a freelance musician, a status which hardly existed when he first started out in the 1750s when a composer not employed by the church or at court was, in truth, unemployed.

Haydn did not have to search hard to find work, and here he was ably assisted by the violinist and impresario Johann Peter Salomon, as well as by a healthy pension from the Esterházys. Haydn traveled with Salomon to London, ready for Salomon's 1791 season of concerts which opened in the Hanover Square Rooms in March. And so Haydn commenced work on his last set of eleven symphonies, his first music written for a paying public, and a venture which was to prove lucrative.

These symphonies are amongst Haydn's most frequently performed music. They include a number of well-known nicknamed works: *No. 94, Surprise*; *No. 96, Miracle*; *No. 100, Military*; *No. 101, Clock*; *No. 103, Drum Roll*; *No. 104, London*. For these, he had at his disposal a group of excellent musicians, an enthusiastic backer, an adoring public, and a supportive press. All of this must have been some kind of culture-shock for Haydn, being in a huge, modern city, compared to his relatively secluded existence at Esterháza in the Austro-Hungarian countryside.

Haydn was a master of invention, so that, of his time at Esterháza, he said that isolation fired his imagination, creativity, and innovation. So too did London, and it is interesting to step back and marvel at just how far he had taken symphonic form. The Morzin and early Esterházy symphonies are inventive within their own worlds. They are written for what today would be described as chamber groups, rather than orchestras in the modern sense, and were listened to by an audience who no doubt chatted, and perhaps ate, throughout the performance. In London, however, Haydn was using the nucleus of what became the modern symphony orchestra. The sound was correspondingly larger, in simple terms louder, than anything he would have heard in the 1750s and 1760s. Moreover, what eventually became known as sonata form had by now become somewhat sophisticated, the ideal vehicle for these relatively large-scale symphonies.

To be sure, and surprisingly, it was only in the second half of the twentieth century that Haydn's true genius was fully appreciated. Until then, relatively few of his symphonies were in the regular repertoire, and he was viewed largely as a genial man producing genial music.

We now know that this is only part of the story, and that Haydn was one of the most innovative of composers, and one of the giants of the eighteenth century. At the time, no one appreciated this more than his younger contemporary, Mozart. In 1798, some years after the latter's death, the Leipzig *Allgemeine Musikalische Zeitung* quoted Mozart as saying, "There is no one who can do it all – to joke and to terrify, to evoke laughter and profound sentiment – and all equally well: except Joseph Haydn."

Mozart

The story of Wolfgang Amadeus Mozart (1756–1791) is the stuff of legends: a child prodigy spending a good deal of his early days touring Europe; feted at royal courts as a young boy; displaying his exceptional keyboard skills to the great, the good, and the not so good; demonstrating his phenomenal musical memory; then a marriage which caused a rift between him and his father; his attempts to become a freelance composer, unheard of at that time; his eventual death at the age of thirty-five; and his burial in an unmarked, pauper's grave.

Between times, he composed dozens of symphonies, more than fifty concertos, twenty-five stage works, an abundance of chamber music, a raft of choral pieces, plus much else. By any standards, he was a prolific composer and, naturally, this section cannot examine in detail any one work. Rather, it aims to offer an overview of the symphonies and concertos, plus a few words on some miscellaneous pieces.

It is fascinating to compare the musical language of Mozart and Haydn. The latter was a considerable influence on Mozart. But there was also mutual esteem, because in his later music, Haydn certainly acknowledges Mozart's skill for writing song-like instrumental lines, and his profusion of melody within sonata form structures. There was, then, some cross-fertilization and, unsurprisingly, many listeners feel there is little differentiation between their styles.

Familiarity with them, however, soon demonstrates obvious lines of stylistic demarcation. For example, Haydn enjoyed constructing themes comprised of smaller motives, rather than Mozart's system of long-breathed melodies. Haydn's development sections are, on the whole, longer than Mozart's, though Haydn is fond of taking a monothematic approach within sonata form structures, where the second subject shares the same theme as the first subject.

Mozart's harmonic language is more chromatic than Haydn's. That said, they were, essentially, using the same idiom, one which had transitioned from the Baroque to the Rococo, and which then became the defining features of the Classical period: the eventual relinquishing of figured bass and continuo; expansion of the orchestra, development of the piano, and the consequent demise of the harpsichord; defining of the symphony and string quartet; expansion of the solo concerto and solo sonata; development of sonata form; less reliance on counterpoint; development, instead, of melody supported by a harmonic accompaniment which contains motivic features derived from the melody itself; more frequent use of dynamic contrasts and other marks of expression.

By the time Mozart started composing his concertos, the concerto grosso was obsolete although, as stated elsewhere, oblique features of it were contained in concertos for two or more soloists, and the sinfonia concertante. The three movement structure of the Baroque concerto remained, but there were considerable differences. Most significantly, the Classical concerto's first movement was cast in an expanded sonata form, rather than the Baroque's ritornello form. This adapted sonata form had a double exposition, the first played by the orchestra alone, and the second for the soloist's entry.

Thus, with few exceptions, the Classical concerto always commences with the orchestra alone, the soloist waiting for this first exposition to run its course before entering. Beethoven was to change this format, and there are Classical exceptions, interestingly, though not radically, in Mozart's *Jeunehomme Concerto*. The device was still being used by composers such as Brahms and Dvořák in the late nineteenth century, and even as late as 1910 in Elgar's *Violin Concerto*.

Another important feature of the Classical concerto, is the inclusion of a solo cadenza towards the end of the first movement. These were not written out, but allowed the soloist to improvise and show off their skill. A shorter cadenza was also usually allowed towards the end of the third movement. From Beethoven onwards, cadenzas were normally written out by the composer, though a late example of an improvised cadenza can be found in Brahms's *Violin Concerto* (1878).

It is interesting to ponder that, apart from a couple of concertos by Haydn, and the odd airing of a concerto by C.P.E. Bach, Mozart's concertos are the only ones from the second half of the eighteenth century which are regularly performed. The repertoire has a wealth of concertos by Bach, Handel and Vivaldi representing the High Baroque, and concertos are part of the supporting pillar of nineteenth century repertoire. This says much about the outstanding quality of Mozart's concertos, compared with others of the period. Of the Mozart concertos, the ones for piano are his finest. The best of these cannot compare with the best of the other concertos, with perhaps the exception of the *Clarinet Concerto* and the *Sinfonia Concertante for Violin and Viola*. However, not all twenty-seven piano concertos are of a consistent quality. The first of any note is *No. 9 in E flat, Jeunehomme* (1777), written for Mlle. Jeunehomme. With its distinguished melodic ideas and lyricism, it looks ahead to the great concertos of the 1780s. It was in this decade that Mozart composed piano concertos of superlative quality.

In the same way that Haydn transformed the symphony from background music to foreground, so too did Mozart change the Classical concerto's emphasis from a display piece, to one which enjoyed the same sense of drama and cohesion as the symphony. Delightful as the *Jeunehomme Concerto* is, it is well to compare it with the tension, pathos and poignancy of the later piano concertos, most notably the two minor key ones, *No. 20 in D minor* (1785), and *No. 24 in C minor* (1786). Beethoven thought highly enough of the *No. 20* to write cadenzas for it, and Mozart's *C minor Concerto* clearly influenced Beethoven's in the same key. Mozart's minor key music is especially affecting, and these two works, along with his *G minor Symphony*, are amongst the most compelling minor key music of the Classical period. Certainly, these later concertos place more emphasis on virtuosity. In some, including the two minor key ones, Mozart uses an expanded orchestra which includes trumpets and timpani, achieving a weightier, indeed more symphonic, sound.

Of the other concertos, there are five for violin, four for horn, concertos for flute, flute and harp, oboe, bassoon, and a *Sinfonia Concertante* for winds. There are also fragments of concertos, arrangements, and attributed compositions. In addition, there is the *Sinfonia Concertante in E flat for Violin and Viola* (1779), and a *Clarinet Concerto in A* (1791), these two works being the best of the non-piano concertos.

The sinfonia concertante form arose during the transition from Baroque to Classical as a hybrid between the concerto grosso, solo concerto and symphony. It enjoyed much popularity amongst composers, including Haydn, who composed them for all manner of instrumental combinations, but Mozart's *Sinfonia Concertante* is by far the finest of them all. In fact, in terms of melodic invention in the first movement alone, and the heartfelt minor key lyricism of the second movement, it leaves his previous concertos standing. Notable, too, is the way in which Mozart's material is so idiomatic and well suited for the dark-hued viola as well as the brighter violin.

The *Clarinet Concerto* was written for the clarinettist Anton Stadler (1753–1812), and was originally conceived for the basset clarinet, an instrument lower in pitch than the standard clarinet, and one which became obsolete almost as soon as Stadler, in conjunction with the instrument maker Theodor Lotz, invented it. The solo parts of the earliest editions of the concerto clearly indicate a basset clarinet part which allows the soloist to use four extra semitones below the clarinet's lowest note. Later editions transpose up the lowest passages for a regular clarinet. This concerto remains one of Mozart's most endearing. It is not particularly virtuosic, but it exploits the rich and mellow colors of the clarinet, supported by a modest size orchestra.

Other works for varying types of ensemble include the assorted divertimenti and serenades. The most famous of these is the *Serenade in G, Eine Kleine Nachtmusik* (1787) for strings, and the massive *Serenade in B flat, Gran Partita* (1781) for thirteen wind instruments. Of additional pieces for full orchestra, are the operatic overtures, which are frequent concert-openers.

The earliest symphonies of Haydn are certainly worth performing. The same cannot be said of Mozart's earliest. The difference is that Haydn was already in his mid-twenties by the time he embarked on his symphonic career, and so he had the musical maturity to carve out a language for himself from the outset. Mozart's early symphonies date from 1765, when he was nine years old and, in truth, are not worth performing, despite their novelty factor. Nonetheless, and not surprisingly, we notice an incremental improvement from here on as the symphonies progress. Eventually we arrive at the *Symphony No. 25 in G minor* (1773), sometimes known as *The Little G minor*, and *No. 27 in A* (1774).

They are his earliest still regularly performed, and there is good reason for this, as they are of a consistent quality throughout, perhaps his most mature works up to date.

The next watershed in Mozart's symphonic output is the *Symphony No. 31 in D, Paris*, composed in 1778 for the Concerts Spirituels in Paris. It proved to be hugely popular for two main reasons. Firstly, the premiere had at its disposal a fine and large orchestra, and the work displays what was then modern and cutting-edge orchestration. With a full set of double woodwind, horns, trumpets, timpani and strings, it was Mozart's largest symphonic orchestra yet, and one which he never exceeded in the later symphonies or concertos. Secondly, its musical gestures contain all that was fashionable, mainly due to what is often known as the Mannheim style, spearheaded by the group of composers in that city, including the Stamitz family.

Thus, in this symphony, we find features typical of the Mannheim School: a rapidly rising melodic figure, as at the symphony's outset, known as the Mannheim sky rocket, though somewhat combined here with the then fashionable Parisian string writing device referred to as *le premier coup d'archet*; extended crescendos; dramatic contrasts of dynamics; tremolando strings; rapid broken chord figuration. Another notable feature of this work is that, unusually for this period, there is no exposition repeat in the first movement.

Mozart's next significant symphonies, before we arrive at the final great trilogy, are the *Symphony No.35 in D, Haffner* (1782), *Symphony No.36 in C, Linz* (1783), and *Symphony No.38 in D, Prague* (1786). Finally, in little over a month in the summer of 1788, Mozart composed his last symphonic masterpieces: *Symphony No.39 in E flat*; *Symphony No.40 in G minor*; *Symphony No.41 in C, Jupiter*, none of which use Mozart's full symphonic orchestra, as benchmarked in the *Paris Symphony*. The significance of these final symphonies is certainly equal to that of Haydn's Salomon symphonies.

In truth there is nothing in the older composer's symphonies which quite matches the dark-hued pathos which opens Mozart's *Fortieth Symphony*. Elements of *Sturm und Drang* there may be in this work, but Mozart's statement here is to transform the intimacy of the string quartet to the more public statement of the symphony. The minuet of the third movement is in name only, for with its cross-rhythms, it defies its dance origins, and its minor key ponderousness relieves it of courtly ancestry, projecting it towards the weighty scherzos of Beethoven.

There are further features which Beethoven adopted. The slow movement, with its quaver up-beat followed by repeated quavers, clearly influenced Beethoven's slow movement in his *First Symphony*. The opening of the *Fortieth* is a rare symphonic example, at this period, of melody being delayed at the expense of accompaniment. Beethoven uses this same procedure to open his *Choral Symphony*, different though the sound-world is. The first movement of the *Thirty-Ninth Symphony* is no less striking for its rare use, in a symphonic first movement at this time, of triple meter, an idea which, again, Beethoven was to exploit in his symphony of the same key, the *Eroica*, a few years later. Beethoven, once more, clearly had his eye on the opening of the *Jupiter* when he came to compose his own *C major Symphony*, which commenced his symphonic career in 1800. The openings of each symphony's *allegro* are too similar to be coincidental.

If, however, one single movement from these three symphonies had to be singled out as an example of a composer defining a new symphonic syntax, then it must be the finale of the *Jupiter*, the most remarkable symphonic movement of the Classical period. It is a fugue, but one combined with sonata form elements. For this reason, and for Mozart's innovative use of the orchestra, the fugal elements sound far from Baroque. The main melodic idea is absurdly simple. But here, simplicity is turned into a virtue, and is diversified to become the basis of a structurally and contrapuntally complex piece.

The fugue has always been the most intricate and cerebral of musical forms, and it is a challenge for any composer to sustain a fugal argument. The inclusion, then, of a complex fugue-type work in a symphony is significant. It lifts the symphony away from the courtly dinner party, and puts it within a realm which places demands on the listener. The *Fortieth Symphony's* minuet makes a similar statement, and in Beethoven's transformation of the minuet to the scherzo, it should not surprise us that the scherzo in his final symphony, the *Choral*, should be fugal.

And so, with the scene now set, with the symphony having come of age under the genius of Haydn and Mozart, the most remarkable symphonies ever were to make their entrance onto the world stage, as we enter the Age of Beethoven.

CHAPTER 3

—

The Age of Beethoven

With Ludwig van Beethoven (1770–1827), we encounter one of the most fascinating of composers. His tempestuous personality, disorderly domestic life and, most significantly, his eventual deafness, present a picture of the archetypal artist, the struggling and striving musician. His nine symphonies and seven concertos represent the central pillar of the orchestral canon, whilst the seventeen string quartets and thirty-two piano sonatas are the mainstay of the recital and chamber repertoire. In addition, his only opera, *Fidelio* (1814) is a heartfelt celebration of freedom and human rights, and his *Mass in D, Missa Solemnis* (1823) is one of the greatest of religious works.

He lived during a period of significant change in Europe. It was an epoch of political and industrial revolution, the age of Napoleon, Goethe, Wordsworth, Constable, Thomas Jefferson and George Washington. The dawn of the railway era, of engineering innovations, of huge industrial cities. It was an exciting and bewildering new world. And here was Beethoven, the first fully self-employed composer.

Ask the proverbial man or woman in the street to sing a snatch of classical music, and the result will invariably be a snippet of Beethoven, more than likely the opening of the *Fifth Symphony in C minor* (1808), but quite possibly also the famous *Ode to Joy* theme from the *Ninth Symphony in D minor, Choral* (1824). Interestingly enough, the *Fifth Symphony's* opening was perhaps the most untuneful symphonic idea to date.

Unlike his predecessors, Beethoven was not overly concerned with the concept of melody *per se* in that opening, but rather with how he could manipulate three short repeated notes followed by one longer note, "fate knocking on the door", as the composer himself described it. A glance at the score of this first movement will readily demonstrate that the Fate rhythm is ubiquitous. In the second movement, it boldly and noticeably surfaces soon after its start, though the opening is preoccupied with melodic line, thereby offering a contrast to the previous movement. In the third movement, the famous rhythm blares out, soon after the hushed opening, and in the Finale, this familiar rhythm might seem hidden, but in fact is offered throughout as a type of rhythmic tag.

Never before had rhythm been used on such an ambitious scale as a unifying feature. So, whilst most people will recognize the opening of this work, it is well to ponder just how far Beethoven had taken the manipulation of rhythm as a means of musical unification. Interestingly, the identical Fate rhythm opens the *Sixth Symphony in F, Pastoral* (1808), but how different the effect is in this rural, pastoral environment of sunny F major, rather than the *Fifth Symphony's* dramatic C minor. It is also as well to consider the impact of the *Fifth Symphony* when it was first performed in 1808. There are countless examples of contemporaries being shocked, bowled over, and declaring Beethoven insane after his premieres.

Exactly what these premieres would have sounded like, is anyone's guess. Orchestral accuracy would have left much to be desired, as unprecedented technical demands were placed on the players. Not only in terms of structure and duration did Beethoven expand and redefine received wisdom on the symphony, but also in the way in which he used the orchestra.

The size of symphony orchestra used was the one Beethoven inherited from Haydn and Mozart in their later works. The *Third Symphony in E flat, Eroica* (1803), adds a third horn to this Classical line-up, though Beethoven reverts back to two horns until the *Choral Symphony*, where he uses two pairs of horns. The *Fifth Symphony* is particularly significant in that three trombones, plus piccolo and double bassoon, make their symphonic debut in the finale. The finale of the *Choral Symphony* additionally includes cymbals, bass drum and triangle, though these instruments can also be found in Haydn's *Military Symphony*, written some thirty years earlier. With the *Choral Symphony*, even without its singers, we arrive at the largest of symphonic forces to date.

Beethoven not only expanded the symphony orchestra, but he placed extra demands on his players. A larger orchestra meant that he was able to achieve a richer and fuller texture than previously. Listen to the finale of the *Fifth Symphony*, and glance at any of its pages to appreciate how far the sound-world had altered since the end of the eighteenth century.

Certainly, there are those places where he was pushing orchestral instruments to the limit of their capabilities for that time, expecting the type of virtuosic playing that is normally the domain of soloists. The cello and bass writing in the Trio section of the *Fifth Symphony's* third movement is a well-known case in point. But there are also those places which, although not technically demanding, produce an altogether different orchestral effect, and the *Pastoral Symphony* is especially rich in these.

Beethoven's instrumental line-up is used sparingly and sensitively in the *Pastoral*. Timpani are employed for just the fourth movement (*Storm*), and here only for forty-five out of one hundred and fifty bars. In the same movement, the piccolo makes its only appearance for a mere twenty-nine bars. The trumpets enter in the third movement (*Peasants Merrymaking*) then stay for the remainder, and the trombones enter in the fourth movement, and stay for the finale.

Perhaps the most memorable passages of orchestration in the whole work, are the bird calls towards the end of the second movement, *Scene by the Brook*. Beethoven actually indicates the assigning of birds to instruments, so that the first flutist becomes a nightingale, the first oboe a quail, and both clarinets, in unison, a cuckoo – or perhaps two cuckoos singing the same song. This oft-quoted passage transcends mere quaintness. It is an early example of a composer making a serious attempt to accurately transcribe birdsong into musical notation, and is therefore not generic birdsong.

The trilling nightingale, the rhythmic quail and the incisive cuckoo are ideally suited to the three instruments chosen, and it would be an interesting exercise to swap the instruments over to demonstrate just how easily the effect would be lost. Beethoven was particularly fond of rural walks and of being amongst nature, and these two identical passages demonstrate just how closely the natural world informed his symphonic thought. Little wonder that, for the Victorians at least, he became the archetypal Romantic.

The string writing in this movement also deserves special attention. The usual five-part strings of two sets of violins, violas, cellos and basses, becomes, in effect, seven parts. Following traditional Classical practice, the cellos and basses play the same line an octave apart. But to add richness, and in an attempt to capture in musical notation the idea of flowing water, Beethoven allocates two separate lines to two solo muted cellos – the violins are also muted, although some editions of the score fail to show this. In Beethoven's day, with fewer string players than in a modern, conventional orchestra, these two cellos would have been more noticeable than in many modern performances. So-called authentic performances of this work demonstrate readily this beautifully calculated orchestration.

Beethoven turns tradition into a virtue here, as there are precedents, notably in Haydn, of the symphonic use of solo strings, concertante-style, as it is sometimes known. But in the *Pastoral*, the solo strings become just a part of the overall texture, rather than soloists in their own right. Beethoven's horn and trumpet writing in the *Pastoral*, is necessarily limited due to these instruments not yet having valves, and therefore being non-chromatic. But genius manifests itself in various guises, and it was there when he decided to end this glorious work with a distant horn call – a muted horn bidding farewell to the unmuted identical horn call that opened the movement.

By the time the 1820s arrived, with the *Choral Symphony* rocketed to fame or infamy, the orchestration innovations announced in the earlier symphonies had become consolidated. So, for example, the timpani tuned in octaves in the second movement was by then not new; Beethoven had discovered octave-tuned timpani in the finale of his *Eighth Symphony in F*, (1812) and was even more daring in his opera *Fidelio* where he threw received wisdom to the wind and tuned them to the tritone. In the *Choral*

Symphony, two pairs of horns in different keys – still natural, without valves – allowed for a greater range of notes than would be the case with one pair. Extra percussion in the finale offered increased brightness and dazzle to an already large orchestra. Added to this, and most obviously, is the use in the finale of a chorus and four solo singers, the first time voices had been heard in a symphony. It enabled Beethoven to set Schiller's *Ode to Joy* and thereby, in effect, it redefined what a symphony is.

The days of the symphony being mere entertainment for one's employer, as was the case with Haydn's wonderfully-crafted symphonies for the Morzin court in the 1760s, were long past. But the world had changed rapidly since then, and Beethoven was writing not for dinner parties in aristocratic rural settings, but for a middle class city-dwelling paying public who were prepared to sit through – not eat through – not twenty, but over sixty or seventy minutes of symphony. After all, by the time the *Choral Symphony* had its premiere, the industrial age was at its height, revolution had swept Europe, and the Napoleonic wars were history.

After the *Choral Symphony's* completion, Beethoven was to enjoy another three years of fertile creativity, producing, most significantly, his final group of string quartets, undoubtedly his most challenging music. He also planned, amongst other things, a tenth symphony, and so it would be wrong to assume that, after the *Choral*, he felt he had said all he had to say in terms of symphonic thought.

Running concurrently with the symphonies are a number of overtures, four of which were written for various versions and revivals of *Fidelio*, others for incidental music for theatrical productions, and a couple as stand-alone works. Apart from the *Fidelio Overture*, which is the 'official' overture to the opera, and the third of the three *Leonore* overtures, which, at one time, conductors occasionally incorporated into the second act of the opera, all the others are now treated as stand-alone concert overtures. Often symphonic in design and drama, they are well-loved orchestral curtain-raisers. At least three of the overtures, *The Ruins of Athens* (1811), *King Stephen* (1811) and *Namesday* (1815), are seldom performed, and for good reason: they contain some of Beethoven's poorest orchestral music, and there is little point in performing second rate Beethoven when overtures such as *Coriolan* (1807), *Egmont* (1810), and the opera overtures are, by any standards, first rate.

The five extant piano concertos contain, like the symphonies, ground-breaking music. It is with the *Fourth Piano Concerto in G* (1806), that Beethoven's experimentation with the genre is perhaps most obvious. By all accounts, Beethoven was a formidable pianist, literally out-playing his rivals. His notoriety as a pianist had a direct influence on piano manufacturing of the day, as the light-actioned instruments became unsuitable for his virtuosic, innovative and increasingly textural piano music. Despite his deafness and the resultant retirement from the concert platform, Beethoven continued to compose solo piano music into the 1820s, though had long ceased to write concertos. In fact, deafness prevented him from premiering his *Fifth* and final concerto.

Beethoven's *Fourth Piano Concerto* is normally cited as the first significant concerto to begin with the soloist alone. It is all too easy to underestimate Beethoven's innovation here. Once again, he makes use of a rhythmic cell which has more than a passing resemblance to the openings of the *Fifth* and *Pastoral* symphonies, with its emphasis on a three-quaver grouping starting on a weak beat. (A similar motive is also employed in the first movement of the *Appassionata Sonata*, and all of these works were written within three years of each other.) Such compositional cross-fertilization between works is not uncommon, even if it might be unintentional or subconscious.

With the *Fourth Piano Concerto's* opening, we have a hushed, gentle, though richly voiced, five-bar phrase in the tonic key of G. The shock factor is with the orchestral strings entering in the sixth bar, even quieter, but in the unexpected and unrelated key of B major. The overall effect, then, is completely different from Mozart's *Jeunehomme Concerto,* which, as previously noted, also opens with the solo piano. With Beethoven, he ensures that his master-stroke has the element of surprise, and hence drama, something which is lacking in the Mozart.

Whilst the first three piano concertos have relatively long middle movements, the slow movements of the later concertos – the last two for piano, the *Violin Concerto in D* (1806) and the *Triple Concerto in C* (1804) – are shorter, with the *Fourth Piano Concerto's* the briefest. Here again, Beethoven is strikingly innovative, and the long, rhapsodic corresponding movements in the earlier concertos seem a stylistic age away. In the *Fourth Piano Concerto*, the slow movement is a dialogue between dramatic, rhythmic and assertive strings, and the contrasting reflective, lyrical and quiet piano part. There is no meeting of minds between the two types of music here; the strings never take up the piano's material, nor vice versa.

For the soloist, this concerto is generally considered to be the most technically demanding of all Beethoven's concertos, though it might not sound it. A perusal of the solo part, however, will look daunting enough to discourage the faint-hearted from attempting any of it. It is fair to observe that it was the most difficult of piano concertos to date, and demonstrates just how far Beethoven had married virtuosity with truly great music, using the increased technical capabilities of an instrument which at that time was in a constant state of development. The influence of such virtuosic writing had its downside, for the nineteenth century is littered with the corpses of long forgotten concertos whose virtuosic content far outweigh compositional value.

Beethoven's concerto legacy also had more positive repercussions, not only in the scope and bold experimentation that was to come with composers such as Liszt and Brahms, but also in the way in which Beethoven treated the orchestra. It still had a supporting role, but he had learned from Mozart that accompaniment need not be bland.

In the *Violin Concerto*, it is not the orchestra, or even the violin, which opens the work, but five quiet crotchet Ds on solo timpani. We have been listening to this concerto for too long in order to fully appreciate this daring stroke. Until Beethoven, timpani had been used mainly as noise-makers, but Beethoven was always keen to experiment with them. In his orchestral music, he increasingly finds more melodic roles for them, so that they are not merely used to reinforce tutti passages.

By opening his *Violin Concerto* in such a way, he emancipates these drums. The opening is not just effect or gimmickry; the timpani rhythm is deftly integrated and used as a unifying motive in the first movement, where it is promoted amongst the rest of the orchestra. In his rarely performed arrangement of this concerto for piano and orchestra, Beethoven composed a fully written out first movement cadenza where the piano is accompanied by the timpani, thereby integrating the idea of solo timpani even more.

The *Fifth Piano Concerto in E flat, Emperor* (1809) takes the *Fourth Piano Concerto's* commencement a stage further. In the *Fifth*, the first sound is a mighty chord on the orchestra, immediately followed by a highly virtuosic written out piano cadenza. Whereas the *Fourth's* opening relied on hushed gentleness and an unexpected change of key, the *Fifth's* is entirely loud, packed with notes, and celebrated in an unambiguous blaze of E flat major. The slow movement, one of the most delicious in the concerto repertoire, is again fairly short, with the accompaniment of muted strings, and a simple melody, creating a mood of quiet reflection. It was not mere whim which persuaded Beethoven to achieve this, but he realized that he needed to have a section of repose between two gigantic and energetic movements. In the *Fourth Piano Concerto*, he arrives at the same goal, though by different means. These are just two examples of how Beethoven achieves long-term balance between movements.

The *Triple Concerto* for piano, violin and cello is noteworthy not for its memorability or strength of character, but for the fact that it was the first time these three soloists had been used within a concerto framework. It is not an entirely successful work, and although it has, not surprisingly, much to commend it, the *Triple Concerto* has not found its way to the hearts of listeners or performers in the same manner as the other concertos.This may be due to an over-long first movement which lacks interesting material to sustain it. Parts of the finale, too, despite its delightful dance-like feel, become formulaic in a way which we do not usually expect in Beethoven.

Also not frequently performed, is the *Choral Fantasia in C* for piano, orchestra and chorus. Completed in 1808 shortly before the *Fifth Piano Concerto*, it is part piano concerto and, in a sense, part preparatory exercise for the finale of the *Ninth Symphony*. Its neglect might be simply due to the fact that the choir is only employed for the final few minutes of what is, in any case, a relatively short work. It might also have something to do with economics: having to engage a concert pianist and a choir. Despite some unimaginative piano writing at its opening, the work never fails to make an effect, and is a wonderful example of Beethoven experimenting, taking compositional risks – and almost pulling it off.

CHAPTER 4

—

The Nineteenth Century (Part I)

Schubert

Beethoven's funeral in March 1827 attracted crowds of thousands. At his death, he was the most famous composer in Europe, and his apparent poverty had more to do with his lack of financial management than his want of fame. Amongst the pallbearers at the funeral, was Franz Schubert (1797–1828) who was himself to die the following year at the age of thirty-one. Schubert died in relative obscurity, his music known only in Vienna. It would be left to the next generation, and in particular composers such as Schumann and Mendelssohn, to discover Schubert's true genius.

It should not surprise us that Schubert was a great admirer of Beethoven. Himself searching for a style in his teens and twenties, Schubert would have devoured Beethoven's music when it became available in print, and would have no doubt attended performances. Schubert's legacy is that of the greatest songwriter of all time. He took the concept of the *Lied*, that art-song peculiar to the Austro-German tradition, rich in the Romantic imagery of contemporary verse, and perfected it.

As a symphonist, however, Schubert struggled, and whilst the earlier symphonies are performed, they identify a composer toiling to find something original to say in the genre. These early works attempt to capture Beethovenian drama, though are essentially products of the late Classical style. It was not death which prevented his *Eighth Symphony in B minor* (1822), known as the *Unfinished*, from completion, but rather his struggle with handling large-scale symphonic form.

Perhaps a lesser composer might have given up, concentrating instead on fewer lengthy works. His *Seventh Symphony* (1821), too, remained unfinished. But he learned from Beethoven, whose symphonies had by now taught him that one does not need to limit oneself to thirty minutes of music in these works. Take a broad canvas of an hour or so, as in the *Eroica* or *Choral* symphonies, and you can express, expand and develop musical ideas in ways undreamed of a generation earlier. It was this Beethoven model that enabled Schubert to complete his final symphony, the *Ninth in C* (1825), the *Great C major* as it is known, to produce one of the finest symphonies of that period.

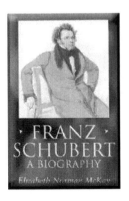

Schubert's scheme for his *Ninth Symphony* is particularly large. In terms of overall structure, it follows the same plan as Beethoven's earlier symphonies, with the slow movement (not really slow as such but, as with the corresponding movement in Beethoven's *Seventh*, with which it shares the same key, it is slow*er*) traditionally coming second, and the Scherzo third. Beethoven's *Ninth* places, for the first time, the slow movement third, an idea taken up by later composers, but not Schubert.

There is also a long slowish introduction to the first movement, though it is not true slow music but, rather, an *Andante*, effortlessly reaching the speed of the *Allegro ma non troppo* proper. Beethoven's slow introductions provided a vital structural process whereby he could set out some of the long-term harmonic and tonal features which would be used later in the movement. But unlike Schubert, he never employed direct thematic quotation from the slow introduction.

Schubert, in his *Ninth Symphony*, breaks with the Beethoven model, which itself had evolved from Haydn and Mozart, and uses the introduction's opening melody as an important and obvious thematic element in his *Allegro* section. Most blatant, and wonderfully executed, is the way in which the opening's soft and lyrical horn call is transformed into a triumphal C major peroration in the closing bars of the movement.

Whether in this sonata form movement, the slow movement, scherzo or finale, Schubert allows the music to unfold not so much leisurely, but in a long-breathed manner. Indeed, Schumann spoke of the "heavenly length" of the second movement. If all the repeats are followed – and they rarely are nowadays – there is about an hour of music.

One might assume that Beethoven's innovation of introducing voices could have appealed to Schubert, whose melodic lines are, not surprisingly, never less than vocal and song-like. Though evidence suggests that Schubert commenced his *Ninth* before Beethoven completed his, the work was not finished until 1828. Moreover, Schubert could express all he wanted to in vocal terms by using his now perfected and intimate *Lied*. In any case, it should come as no revelation that symphonic composers in the period immediately following Beethoven's *Ninth* felt necessarily intimidated by what seemed to be a symphony of symphonies, and a controversial one at that.

The early performers of Schubert's *Ninth Symphony* – it was first heard, thanks to Schumann, though conducted by Mendelssohn, in 1839 – found the instrumental writing to be especially daunting and tiring, due to rapid repeated notes for the woodwinds, and long passages of repeated figuration for the strings. Schubert's scoring in this work not only reflects the innovations that Beethoven had made but, in some respects, goes beyond this, though his orchestras are never larger than Beethoven's.

For example, whereas Beethoven is sparing in his use of trombones, Schubert employs them throughout his *Ninth Symphony*, taking full advantage of the fact that he has the luxury of three wholly chromatic instruments within his brass group. He not merely uses the trombones to add drama and weight in loud tutti passages, but also exploits their mellow characteristics in quieter, chamber-like passages. Put into perspective, we should remember that, unlike Beethoven, Schubert could actually hear what trombonists were now capable of in the 1820s.

Without the *Great C major*, Schubert would still be remembered as a giant amongst nineteenth century composers on account of his songs. With this symphony alone, he stands with the greatest as a supreme symphonist.

Rossini, Weber and Paganini

Perhaps it is because of Beethoven towering over the period, that very little orchestral music from the first thirty years of the nineteenth century remains in the regular repertoire. The overtures of Gioachino Rossini (1792–1868), all of them written in Beethoven's lifetime, are performed frequently, and make for effective and colorful concert openers, carefully crafted and imaginatively orchestrated as they are.

Some of the orchestral music of Carl Maria von Weber (1786–1826) is performed, and deservedly so. These include the two particularly fine *Clarinet Concertos* (1811), the *Concertino for clarinet and orchestra* (1811), and the overtures to *Der Freischütz* (1821) and *Oberon* (1826). The violin concertos of the formidable virtuoso violinist Niccolo Paganini (1782–1840) are occasionally performed, but although their solo parts are dazzling, the musical material itself, and the orchestration is, in the main, dull.

Berlioz

As the 1820s gave way to the next decade, the Frenchman Hector Berlioz (1803–1869) completed his *Symphonie Fantastique* in 1830. It remains one of the most astonishing and original symphonies of the nineteenth century. The story surrounding its composition, the program, or narrative that Berlioz provided, and which the music follows, has perhaps, for the concertgoer, eclipsed the astounding invention of the music itself. The work's original title was *Episodes in the Life of an Artist*, telling of the artist's love for a woman, resulting in emotional extremes, the artist murdering his lover, and eventual execution.

Taking his lead from Beethoven's *Pastoral Symphony*, with which it shares some common ground, the *Symphonie Fantastique* has five movements. They are subtitled: *Daydreams – Passions*; *A ball*; *In the Meadows*; *March to the Scaffold*; *Sabbath Night's Dream*. In fact, there is some element of autobiography here, as Berlioz had become infatuated with the Irish Shakespearean actress, Harriet Smithson. Love unrequited brought him much despair, though they eventually married.

Nineteenth century music was to be characterized, to some extent, by program music. It was not, of course, a new phenomenon. Examples can be found from the Renaissance through to Beethoven's *Pastoral Symphony*, via Vivaldi's *The Four Seasons* and Haydn's use of program within a symphony.

Yet the *Symphonie Fantastique* was the first time that an extensive and detailed narrative was applied to each movement, and it was the composer's intention that this should be printed in the concert program for each performance. This marriage of symphonic thought and program became an aesthetic in its own right for Berlioz, and was highly innovative.

The second innovation in this work, is the relinquishing of Classical symphonic form. There is something of a paradox here, as Berlioz was obsessed with the music of Beethoven, a composer whose own innovations were a direct result of a re-evaluation of the Classical style. Yet it was Beethoven's willingness to experiment and take compositional risks which so appealed to Berlioz. The third movement, *In the Meadows*, has its obvious parallels with Beethoven's *Pastoral Symphony*.

The second movement is a waltz. Just as the democratic Beethoven discarded the courtly minuet, replacing it with the rhythmic scherzo, thereby making a political statement by removing the symphony as the preserve of the aristocracy, so Berlioz introduced, in his second movement, the waltz into the symphony. This dance was seen as somewhat risqué in its day, not only because of the physical intimacy it brought to the dancers, but because it was not limited to a monied upper class; it became a dance for the increasingly influential middle class.

The way in which Berlioz renounced the sonata form symphonic tradition, is by his use of a recurrent theme, the *idée fixe*, in all the movements, thereby acting as a compositional unifying feature. Beethoven had, of course, used motives to achieve unity as, for example, in the *Fifth Symphony*. The *idée fixe*, however, is more than a motive; it is a forty-bar theme. It was Berlioz's invention, and by using it, he could attain unity without having recourse to employ sonata form to build a symphonic argument. The third innovation is in the realm of orchestration. Berlioz was one of the most imaginative orchestrators of the century, and in fact wrote a textbook on the subject. Harp, cor anglais, E flat (piccolo) clarinet, cornet (a new instrument at the time) and orchestral bells all make their symphonic debut in the *Symphonie Fantastique*.

In addition, chords on timpani are employed, as well as two timpanists. There are, occasionally, multiple divisions in the string section, including chords played by the double bass section, and *col legno* (with the back of the bow) for the violins. The percussion section, apart from timpani, until then used mainly to add color and noise, if used at all, has now been promoted almost as an equal with the other sections.

Even Berlioz must have felt that the *Symphonie Fantastique* was a hard act to follow, and his second symphony – Berlioz did not number his symphonies – is on a more modest scale. *Harold in Italy* (1834) is not a lesser work, but it is different. Byron's *Childe Harold* is the starting point here, represented by the solo viola so that, in effect, the symphony becomes akin to a programmatic viola concerto. Less startling, understandably less innovative, but no less well crafted than the *Symphonie Fantastique*, *Harold in Italy* is obviously descriptive, and once again employs the *idée fixe* device.

His third symphony is the gigantic *Romeo and Juliet Symphony* (1839), subtitled *A dramatic symphony*. Unlike the other symphonies, it is infrequently performed, and has been criticized for its attempt to marry two types of drama, one symphonic, the other operatic. But, in fact, here is where its innovation and genius can be found. Any performance of this work is an ambitious project, and its neglect might have more to do with its length, rather than any compositional miscalculations.

Mendelssohn

It would be difficult to think of two contemporary composers more dissimilar than Berlioz and Felix Mendelssohn (1809–1847). Berlioz the experimenter, who struggled long and hard to gain recognition, offered a symphonic view which was far removed from the Austro-German Classical symphonic tradition. Mendelssohn, on the other hand, was born into a wealthy Hamburg family – his grandfather being the great Jewish philosopher Moses Mendelssohn – and was content to inherit genres as bequeathed by Beethoven.

He was also a child prodigy viewed, certainly by his family, as something of a second Mozart. But here is the interesting thing. Whereas the music he was producing in his teens was as good as, and even better than, much that was being written in the 1820s, Mendelssohn's style did not fundamentally change. Unlike so many great composers, it did not mature as he got older, he merely consolidated it, so that, for instance, the *Midsummer Night's Dream Overture* (1826), really is as good as, say, the *Violin Concerto in E minor* (1844). In keeping with Berlioz, though, and with the spirit of the age, Mendelssohn's muse was directly informed by program music, be it his programmatic overtures or the *Italian* and *Scottish* symphonies. Despite the fact that his style did not significantly alter, that he was not a great innovator or risk taker, he was nonetheless something of a genius.

Mendelssohn composed five symphonies in total (not including those of juvenilia), but it is only the last two, the *Symphony in A, Italian* (1833) and the *Symphony in A minor, Scottish* (1842), which are regularly performed, though choral societies are quite fond of his choral symphony, *The Hymn of Praise* (*Lobgesang*, 1840). These two popular symphonies, with the *Italian* being one of the most admired of any symphonies, are not overtly programmatic in the narrative way of Berlioz's *Symphonie Fantastique*, but their starting point was largely due to a European grand tour undertaken by the composer between 1829 and 1832. Even so, Mendelssohn said that the opening of the *Scottish* was inspired by his visit to the ruined chapel at Edinburgh's Holyrood Palace, the second movement of the *Italian* is a pilgrims' march, whilst its finale is based on the rhythm of a Roman dance, the *saltarello*.

Beyond this, the symphonies are far less descriptive than the much loved *Hebrides (Fingal's Cave) Overture* (1830), where the listener's imagination can easily conjure up images of undulating waves, stormy sea and cavernous cave. Mendelssohn's reputation as one of the great composers of the nineteenth century rests on only a few works, which says much about his genius and craftsmanship.

Additional to the orchestral works already mentioned, there is the popular overture (1826) and incidental music (1843) to *A Midsummer Night's Dream*, the overture *Ruy Blas* (1839), and the *Octet* for strings which is often played by a full string orchestra. The *Piano Concerto in G minor* occasionally receives an airing. In addition to these works is the intensely lyrical *Violin Concerto*, one of the most frequently performed concertos in the repertoire.

Mendelssohn's use of form and structure is never less than craftsmanlike, possibly due to the fact that, like Handel or Mozart, he made few preliminary sketches for his works. In any case, he was using received forms, and sonata form was, after all, by the 1830s tried and tested. Consequently, there is always a fine sense of spontaneity. One need listen no further than the *Italian Symphony* or *Violin Concerto* to appreciate this. These works will also demonstrate the song-like lyricism that many of his melodies enjoy; like Schubert, he was a fine songwriter, though lacking Schubert's sense of innovation.

Mendelssohn had a special flair for orchestration, while he never used particularly large orchestras. The *Italian* and *Scottish* symphonies do not use orchestras significantly larger than the later works of Haydn or Mozart, or some of the earlier Beethoven symphonies. But the felicitous touches of orchestration and his sensitivity towards this could warrant a separate chapter in its own right. His orchestration was not daring, and he did not do anything that his contemporaries were not doing. But in his own way, he was as fine an orchestrator as Berlioz and, as we shall see, better than his contemporary symphonist, Schumann. Had Handel, Wagner, Brahms, Verdi or Elgar died at the same age as Mendelssohn – thirty-eight – they would have received far fewer column inches in music history books than Mendelssohn enjoys.

Schumann

Mendelssohn's friend and compatriot Robert Schumann (1810–1856) was the embodiment of the German Romantic school of the first half of the nineteenth century. His devotion to contemporary German Romantic literature had a direct influence on the often programmatic and whimsical characteristics of his music. Along with Schubert, he is recognized as one of the great song writers of the century, and his piano music is part of the mainstay of the repertoire. Whilst many of his songs and piano pieces are perfect examples within their genres, even the most ardent of Schumann's admirers would agree that the same cannot be said about the orchestral music.

There can be no doubt, however, about his best loved orchestral work, the *Piano Concerto in A minor*, in its final form completed in 1845. Symphonic in approach, its material is tightly argued and tautly handled, with brilliant piano writing which never lapses into virtuosity for virtuosity's sake. This cannot be overstated in a century which was burdened with countless concertos, all trying to outdo each other in virtuosic dazzle at the expense of musical argument.

By comparison, his two other concertos are somewhat neglected. The *Cello Concerto in A minor* (1850) has always been passed over in favor of the *Piano Concerto*, despite having much to commend it. The neglect of the *Violin Concerto*, suppressed after Schumann's death, and not performed until the 1930s, is hardly surprising. It was his last completed composition, written in 1853 during his final mental illness when his critical faculty as a composer had all but evaporated. Far more successful is the concerto-like *Concertstück* (1849) for four horns and orchestra, a rare and brilliant example of a solo horn ensemble with orchestra.

There are issues with the four symphonies. Whilst they form part of the standard orchestral repertoire, none of them have enjoyed the same popularity as Mendelssohn's *Italian* or *Scottish* symphonies. Within them, though, is some remarkable music. The *Fourth Symphony in D minor* perhaps demonstrates well Schumann's struggle to solve symphonic intricacies. He originally had the idea to call it *Symphonic Fantasy*, for reasons that will become apparent, and the first version of the work was written in 1841. He then radically revised it ten years later, and it is this version which is played today. This is a pity, as the first version is generally preferable, due to more translucent and, by and large, lighter scoring.

And hereby hangs a problem which haunts Schumann's orchestral music. Unlike Mendelssohn, he was not a master orchestrator. His woodwind writing lacks light and shade, offering little scope for individual soloists within the group to shine, and his string writing too often attempts to emulate piano figuration. His horn writing can lead to problems with orchestral balance, and too much emphasis is placed on doubling melodic lines, so that textures can become over-scored. These problems are especially apparent in the *Fourth Symphony's* second version, where excessive doublings of parts was perhaps an attempt to compensate for the relatively poor ensemble of the Düsseldorf orchestra which premiered it in 1853.

The 1851 version of this symphony does have advantages over the earlier version, however. It contains a new transition from the slow introduction to the main part of the first movement and, most significantly, it contains a bold and magnificent transition linking the third movement to the finale, which may have influenced the introduction to the finale in Brahms's *First Symphony*. Poor orchestration notwithstanding, the *Fourth Symphony*, with its four movements played without a break, and use of cyclic form where material is reintroduced throughout to achieve an excellent sense of unity, is startlingly original. In a sense, the work is something of a hybrid, attempting, as it does, to marry Berlioz's *idée fixe* with Beethovenian logic. Because of its cyclic form, Schumann no doubt felt more comfortable with an initial working title which linked symphony with fantasy. But the title *Symphony* eventually prevailed, and this work remains Schumann's most daring foray in the genre.

The other symphonies contain a wealth of fine ideas, even if large-scale and long-term symphonic development of material is sometimes lacking. The *Third Symphony in E flat, Rhenish* (1850) is, overall, perhaps Schumann's most successful and powerful. Following Beethoven's model in the *Pastoral Symphony*, it is cast in five movements, and is the closest any of these symphonies come to being program music. But its opening has more in common with Beethoven's *Eroica Symphony*, with its striding and assertive arpeggio-based main theme, itself perhaps going on to influence the openings of Brahms's *Third* and Elgar's *Second* symphonies.

The fourth movement is one of those moments in Schumann's symphonies when we realize why these works, like the proverbial curate's egg, excellent in parts, have stood the test of more than one hundred and fifty years. Said to conjure up a solemn ceremony in Cologne Cathedral, this majestic, chorale-type movement, with its somber and dramatic trombones and Bach-like pacing, is one of the most noble and carefully calculated passages in these four symphonies.

Chopin and Liszt

Apart from program music being on the ascendancy in the nineteenth century, it was also the age of the virtuoso. Audiences expected more and more virtuosity from performers, and the cult of the solo virtuoso was born. Even in the early years of the century, pianistic duals were fought between pianists, Beethoven amongst them, all of whom tried to out-play each other. Piano music became more and more technically demanding, and pianos became sturdier in order to cope with this. Nor was this phenomenon restricted to the piano. Audience reaction at violinist Paganini's concerts was something akin to Beatlemania in the 1960s.

The two greatest composer-pianists in the first half of the century were both from eastern Europe: Frederic Chopin (1810–1849) from Poland, and the Hungarian Franz Liszt (1811–1886).

There is nothing in Chopin's catalog of works which does not include the piano. Much of it is for solo piano, and these works are amongst the most frequently played piano pieces of all time. He composed two piano concertos, the *First in E minor*, and the *Second in F minor*, both relatively early works, composed between 1829 and 1830. Delightful and popular though they are, these are not ground-breaking compositions. They are essentially Classical in form, with orchestral accompaniments which are, in the main, pedestrian.

It would be left to Liszt in his two piano concertos to re-examine concerto form. Chopin gave relatively few public concerts. Liszt, on the other hand, invented the concept of the solo piano recital. It was he, for example, who first performed all the Beethoven sonatas as a cycle of recitals. He had good reason to do this, for not only was he greatly influenced by Beethoven in general, but his teacher, Carl Czerny, was a pupil of Beethoven. Liszt himself, as a prodigious eleven year-old, was introduced by his teacher to Beethoven.

By all accounts, Liszt's piano playing was phenomenal. Like Paganini, he had great presence on the concert platform. In his younger days, attractive, with charisma and sex appeal, his recitals caused a sensation, resulting in hysterics and swoons from women in particular. His music was as innovatory as his playing, and his piano works are amongst the most significant in the repertoire.

Like Berlioz, he experimented with form and thematic development which led him, eventually, to invent the symphonic poem, a form well utilized by later composers. Something of a hybrid linking the programmatic symphony to the programmatic concert overture, Liszt's twelve symphonic poems attempt a re-enactment in music of a story or drama. Only *Les Préludes*, and perhaps *Mazeppa* are performed today, and at that infrequently.

In addition, he also composed two symphonies, the choral *Faust Symphony* (1854), dedicated to Berlioz, and the *Dante Symphony* (1856), dedicated to Wagner. Again, these can hardly be described as staples of the orchestral repertoire. The *Faust Symphony*, despite its neglect, is one of the most important symphonies of the period. Ambitious in scale, Liszt struggled to bring it to a form that he was satisfied with. In fact, the 1854 version was one of three. He had already sketched some of it in the 1840s, and then revised it extensively in 1861, and added some further revisions as late as 1880. It is also one of the first works that he scored entirely himself, as earlier orchestral works were usually scored by others.

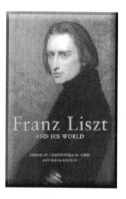

But, having obviously worked hard on this aspect, there can be no denying the effectiveness of the orchestration. We should not underestimate Liszt's flair for experimentation, despite the neglect of much of his orchestral music. In the first version of the *Faust Symphony*, for example, there are passages in 7/4 and 7/8 time which, for its day, was cutting-edge metrical notation. These meters were later ironed out, so to speak, into conventional simple-time.

By comparison with the purely orchestral music, the two piano concertos, both composed in 1848, are amongst the most frequent to be heard on the concert platform. In both the *First Piano Concerto in E flat*, and *Second Piano Concerto in A*, which was revised in 1856, there is the same sense of thematic unity and transformation of themes that we find in the orchestral works. Added to this is some of the most virtuosic piano writing to be found in any concerto. They are also amongst the shortest of nineteenth century concertos, largely due to the concentrated way in which Liszt develops material and handles form. For example, the *A major Concerto* is cast in one continuous, unified movement, with sub-sections.

These concertos are especially significant, in that they marry high-velocity virtuosity with innovative, finely-crafted musical ideas, and effective orchestration. This should not be underestimated when compared to the numerous justly neglected nineteenth century concertos where soloistic pyrotechnics were always at the expense of musical argument.

CHAPTER 5

—

The Nineteenth Century (Part II)

Wagner

Liszt's son-in-law, Richard Wagner (1813–1883), is chiefly remembered for his daring vision which transformed nineteenth century opera. His purely orchestral works – the early *Symphony in C* (1832), and the *Faust Overture* (1855) – play no significant role in a discussion of the century's orchestral repertoire. The only exception is the beautiful *Siegfried Idyll*, composed in 1870 as a birthday gift to his wife, Cosima, Liszt's daughter. Cosima had recently given birth to their son, Siegfried, though the work's title is doubly significant, as the *Idyll* quotes music from Wagner's opera *Siegfried*, which was work-in-progress at the time. The *Siegfried Idyll*, scored for chamber orchestra, demonstrates that Wagner was not only capable of producing his huge operas, or music dramas, as he preferred to call them, but also delicately structured chamber music.

There are many orchestral extracts from the operas which are in the regular repertoire. These include the overtures to *Rienzi* (1842), *The Flying Dutchman* (1843), *Tannhäuser* (1845), *The Mastersingers* (1868), and the preludes to *Lohengrin* (1850), *Tristan and Isolde* (1859) and

Parsifal (1882). In addition, there are various orchestral extracts from his group of four operas (*The Rhinegold, The Valkyrie, Siegfried, Twilight of the Gods*) known as *The Ring*, completed in 1876, the *Venusberg* music from *Tannhäuser*, and the concluding scene, the *Liebestod*, from *Tristan and Isolde*.

The great orchestral passages in Wagner's operas are not merely curtain-raisers or interludes; they are equal to the vocal passages in terms of musical invention. But out of all of them, the *Prelude* to *Tristan and Isolde* is by far the most significant when considering the development of nineteenth century music. Here, Wagner seems to be on the threshold of a new musical language where traditional tonality and harmonic progressions are being challenged; where the sense of tonality, aided by what is known as the *Tristan* chord – indefinable by Classical nomenclature – is nebulous, and where discords, rather than resolving, melt into a chain of other discords. The music might not seem particularly shocking to our millennium ears, but we should not underestimate the impact that it had on both audiences and composers alike. It led, eventually, for example, for composers like Richard Strauss, Mahler and, in particular, Arnold Schoenberg, to reassess received wisdom on the concept of key and tonality.

In many ways, Wagner was an unpleasant individual. One does not need to be a saint in order to produce great art, and notwithstanding his vicious and obsessive anti-Semitism, Wagner was undoubtedly the most influential composer of his generation and, along with Berlioz, the most experimental in his use of the orchestra.

Bruckner

To some extent, Anton Bruckner (1824–1896) was something of a maverick, so much so that his influence has been minimal. As an individual, he was rather a loner, and this manifests itself in his music, which stands somewhat apart from that of his contemporaries. He was deeply religious, and his impressive chorale-like, organ-textured, churchy melodies, especially in his slow movements, remain a touching, if not to some extent naïve, testimony to his piety. Whilst some of his choral music is regularly performed, he is almost exclusively remembered as the composer of eight completed symphonies, plus an unfinished ninth. Unlike Brahms, his symphonies are not rooted to Classical forms. Their epic length, chromatic language and orchestration owe something to Wagner, whilst their lyricism harks back to Schubert. Beyond this, Bruckner viewed the symphonies of Beethoven as the creative ideal, and to a large extent, his symphonic quest was to assimilate Beethoven's grand designs in order to produce an original, late nineteenth century symphonic vision.

Bruckner's music was slow to gain recognition outside of Austria and Germany. Even today, music lovers and musicians are often divided in their views on him. On the one hand, there are those who believe him to be, without question, one of the greatest of symphonists. On the other hand, some consider him to be no more than a talented amateur, struggling, but ultimately failing, to handle large scale symphonic form. It is these people who, perhaps unkindly, have commented that Bruckner did not write nine symphonies, but one symphony nine times. There is a grain of truth in this, as the basic character and sound-world differs little from symphony to symphony. Be that as it may, it does not necessarily offer a fair value judgement on the composer.

The one work which influenced Bruckner above all others, was Beethoven's *Ninth Symphony*, the *Choral*. Though Bruckner never composed a choral symphony, it was the basic design of Beethoven's *Choral Symphony* which so intrigued him. It was not until Bruckner moved to Linz in 1856 that he became more familiar with Beethoven's music, and even then he did not produce his first mature symphony until he was in his forties.

What impressed Bruckner most about the *Choral Symphony* was its huge first movement with its granite-like blocks of sound, an extensive and vigorous scherzo, a large-scale slow movement, and a vast, summarizing finale. This is the Bruckner model, though whereas Beethoven recalls in his finale the themes from earlier movements and discards them, Bruckner is keen, in his final pages, to conclude his symphonies with his opening idea. Bruckner's slow movements are certainly Beethovenian in scope and structure and, arguably, remain the finest features of his symphonies.

It was the opening of Beethoven's *Ninth*, however, which so fascinated Bruckner. Beethoven's opening sounds like a slow introduction, in truth a brilliant deception, for it carries an *Allegro* tempo marking. But there is little rhythmic interest, and the slow harmonic rhythm – the rate of change of the harmonies – seems to slow everything down. What Beethoven is actually doing is amassing fragments of material which will constitute his first main theme. It was a startlingly original idea. Bruckner took this concept and tried to produce a similar, though original, effect to open his symphonies. In one sense, he failed, simply because Beethoven had already done it. Yet in another sense, it was a true challenge for Bruckner because, certainly, he was the first composer who attempted to confront and assimilate Beethoven's opening.

If we consider any of the openings of symphonies by the three composers discussed immediately below, we notice that in every instance, and notwithstanding slow introductions or, as in Tchaikovsky's case, motto themes, they launch straight in to a fully-fashioned melody. Bruckner's use of fragmented ideas which are then gathered into a theme, was an inventive and admirable response to the opening to Beethoven's *Ninth*.

Where these openings fall down, it could be argued, is in Bruckner's use, time and again, of this formula: tremolo strings and reliance of broken-chord, slow fanfare-type figuration. For Bruckner, though, it was the ideal vehicle for him to gradually develop his material in an organic way. For many, the most memorable features of the symphonies are the long-breathed slow movements, with those from the *Fourth Symphony in E flat, Romantic* (1874, revised 1878 and 1880), *Seventh Symphony in E* (1883), and *Eighth Symphony in C minor* (1887, revised 1890), being particularly fine. A composer much admired by Hitler, the *Eighth Symphony's* slow movement is somewhat tainted by the fact that it was broadcast on German radio on the announcement of Hitler's death.

Bruckner's symphonies have grown in popularity over the years, but it is a popularity rather different from that enjoyed by the symphonies of his contemporaries to be discussed below. The symphonies certainly make demands on the listener, not merely because of their great length, but because there is a certain seriousness, indeed gloominess, to them. Whilst they have never achieved the iconic status of those by Brahms, there is no denying their artistic integrity and unquestionable technique.

Brahms

With Johannes Brahms (1833–1897), we arrive at one of the greatest symphonists since Beethoven. Although he wrote just four symphonies, they remain, along with Beethoven's, the supporting pillars of the symphonic repertoire. Unlike Wagner, Brahms eschewed opera; unlike Berlioz, Liszt or Mendelssohn, he avoided program music. Apart from his songs and choral music, including *A German Requiem*, Brahms's many chamber works, symphonies and four concertos represent the century's apogée of what is sometimes referred to as absolute music, music without any reference to programmatic elements. Brahms and

Wagner were viewed in their day as being the two great opposing forces in contemporary Austro-German music. Indeed, quite often, critics allied themselves with either one or the other. Yet despite their opposing aesthetics, both were profoundly influenced by Beethoven in terms of the expansion of genres and the handling of large scale structures.

Unlike Wagner, Brahms avoided the use of huge resources in his orchestral works. For example, his employment of extra percussion, in addition to timpani, is rare. He seldom engaged a harp, and whilst trombones appear in all four symphonies, they are utilized sparingly, and are not required in any of the four concertos. The *Second Symphony in D* (1877) is an infrequent example of Brahms's employment of the tuba.

His orchestration has occasionally, and unfairly, come under some criticism for its lack of light and shade, and for its muddy and thick textures. In fact, the textures are not muddy and thick but, rather, rich and sonorous. Moreover, one need only look at the third movement of this *Second Symphony*, and second movement of the *Third Symphony in F* (1883) to discover chamber-like, delicate orchestration offering effective dialogue between sections of the orchestra, and thereby contributing towards a wonderful sense of contrasts.

Brahms has often been described as the Classical Romantic. In other words, although he was writing within what is known as the Romantic period, his compositional outlook was essentially Classical in the way in which he handled structure, and in the genres he used. His *First Symphony in C minor* (1876) was, in fact, hailed by critics as *Beethoven's Tenth*, as many saw it as a worthy successor to Beethoven's monumental *Ninth Symphony*. Less kind critics also branded it as *Beethoven's Tenth*, asserting that the work was nothing more than re-labelled Beethoven. It is true that Brahms never lost sight of his Classical heritage. Indeed, his influences go further back, for example acknowledging the Baroque, and Bach in particular, in the remarkable passacaglia finale to his *Fourth Symphony in E minor* (1885).

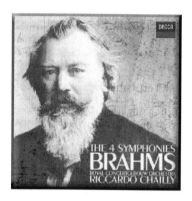

Instantly recognizable in Brahms's music, are the Classical shapes of his melodic lines, due largely to simple melodic ideas which are triadically based. There are countless examples of this type of melodic shaping in Haydn, Mozart and Beethoven, but perhaps less so as the nineteenth century progressed and where increasing chromaticism, as in Liszt or Wagner, was less able to support firmly diatonic and triadic melodies. Obvious examples in Brahms's music are the themes which open his *Second Symphony*, the *Violin Concerto* and the *First Piano Concerto*.

Such was his integration of the Classical style, that Brahms was to easily assimilate this into his exquisitely constructed *Variations on a Theme by Joseph Haydn* (1873), sometimes known as *Variations on the St. Anthony Chorale*, though it is now almost certain that the theme itself is not by Haydn. Here, Brahms was writing a set of variations on a Classical theme, with the variations themselves Classical in design along with their melodic manipulation and, to some extent, orchestration, yet expressed within late nineteenth century musical language. This is a particularly effective example of Brahms the Classical Romantic.

The *Fourth Symphony* is possibly Brahms's summation of his assimilation of Classical, and also Baroque, design. Its opening might sound arpeggio-based, and deceptively Classical. Yet closer examination reveals that the melody is, in fact, a chain of descending thirds. This is a particularly un-Classical idea, for the Classical masters would simply not have employed such a huge span of thirds without having some conjunct movement between notes. Typical of the way in which Brahms integrates material, and a procedure which puts him in direct line of descent from Beethoven, are the techniques by which the interval of a third, prevalent in the work's opening, becomes a unifying feature within the rest of the symphony. In the opening of the second movement, for instance, the melody never rises nor falls more than a third.

The *Fourth Symphony* is the only one of the Brahms set which includes a movement that approaches anything like a Beethoven scherzo. In the other symphonies, Brahms preferred to have lighter intermezzo-like, chamber-type movements, in addition to his slow movements. The general atmosphere in the *Fourth Symphony* is somewhere between lyricism, as in the first movement's first subject, and somberness.

The scherzo-like third movement certainly helps to add some gaiety to the proceedings before the weighty finale, and in fact Brahms's tempo indication of *Allegro* adds the word *Giocoso*.

The fourth and final movement of this remarkable work is a set of variations based on an eight-bar chaconne theme which Brahms took, and slightly modified, from Bach's *150th Cantata*. Above and below this theme, and within a timeframe of only around eleven minutes, Brahms constructs thirty variations and a coda, modelled on the passacaglia principle – a variation device widely using during the Baroque.

There is a paradox within this movement, a canny trick, for it feels and sounds like music built on a huge scale, but yet in reality is his shortest symphonic finale. This deception is achieved by Brahms's concentration of his material, where there seem to be no extraneous notes in this tightly argued structure. Within, there are two passages, following close on the heels of each other, which bring the listener to the spiritual heart of this symphony. The music by now has slowed down, and the first of these two passages is the twelfth variation, where a solo flute muses on the main theme, and where its eloquence recalls the more expressive and reflective arias from Bach's *St. Matthew Passion*. The second passage is two variations later, where the trombones re-enter, not having been heard since the second variation, and where they now offer a sarabande-like chorale, complete with gentle discords. The chaconne melody suddenly and dramatically breaks this reflective interlude, the final set of variations are ushered in, and the powerful coda brings to a close one of the most deceptively original symphonies since Beethoven.

Though he was to live another twelve years, Brahms did not return to the symphony, perhaps feeling that he had said all he wanted to within his perceived idea of the post-Beethoven symphony. In any case, his remaining years saw Mahler compose his first three symphonies, and so, it would seem, a new symphonic age had begun. Brahms did not entirely turn his back on large scale orchestral music, however. His symphonies may have been completed, but he had not yet finished the last of his four concertos.

Like the symphonies, the two piano concertos, *Violin Concerto* and *Double Concerto for Violin and Cello* are large-scale works, and are amongst the most frequently performed of any works in this genre. The *Double Concerto in A minor* (1887) was Brahms's last substantial orchestral work. Why it has remained his least performed concerto, is anyone's guess, though, in practical terms, it could have something to do with it needing two virtuosos rather than one.

Brahms's first concerto was the *First Piano Concerto in D minor*, which started life in 1853 as sketches for a symphony. It indicates that Brahms thought naturally in terms of symphonic conception, though the *First Symphony* itself had a gestation period of almost twenty years. A sonata for two pianos was the next stage in the *First Piano Concerto's* development until, in 1861, it achieved its final form. Highly virtuosic, it is still a daunting play for even today's breed of super-pianists, which perhaps gives some indication of Brahms's own prowess as a pianist. With its exuberance and drama, this concerto is certainly the work of a relatively young composer who has finally arrived at his own distinctive style. In form and structure, it is indebted to Classical models, and Beethoven in particular. The rondo finale, for example, contains a fugato passage which was clearly influenced by a similar passage in the finale of Beethoven's *Third Piano Concerto*. Like a Classical concerto, its first movement opens with an orchestral exposition before the soloist enters; of all the Brahms concertos, only his *Second Piano Concerto in B flat*, composed some twenty-two years later, breaks with this tradition.

The *Violin Concerto in D* (1878) also demonstrates Brahms's allegiance to the Classical ideal in allowing the soloist to improvise a first movement cadenza, a feature which many composers had dispensed with a generation earlier. This work is often cited as the last concerto to permit this feature.

All the concertos contain long-breathed slow movements, with the *Double Concerto's* being shortest. Listening to the opening of the *Violin Concerto's* slow movement, one might be forgiven into thinking that the music had strayed into an oboe concerto, for Brahms offers us twenty-five slow bars of a sublimely lyrical oboe solo before the violin enters after a well-earned rest following the taxing first movement. Brahms employs a similar device in the opening of the slow third movement in the *Second Piano Concerto* where, this time, a solo cello weaves through the introduction before the piano steals in. The *Second Piano Concerto* remains amongst the repertoire's most monumental concertos. Cast in four movements, it is, for the soloist, undoubtedly one of the most exhausting of works in this genre. It has often been described as a symphony with piano obligato. Indeed, its second movement is a truer scherzo than anything found in the Brahms symphonies. It was Brahms's answer to transporting the Beethoven symphonic scherzo into the concerto, complete with a neo-baroque Handelian-like trio section.

Brahms's two concert overtures, both written in 1880, demonstrate two sides to his musical personality. The *Tragic Overture* is a dramatic, at times gloomy work, as ambitious as a symphonic first movement. The *Academic Festival Overture*, by contrast, is a skilfully woven *potpourri* of student songs dressed up in some of Brahms's most colorful orchestration. It belongs more to the lighter side of his output, along with his *Waltzes* and *Hungarian Dances*. There are also two orchestral suites, infrequently performed and, unlike any of the other orchestral music, unable to sustain interest in quite the same way.

Like Beethoven before him, and similar to Mahler and Sibelius who were to follow, Brahms is one of the few composers whose almost every orchestral work is frequently performed. At a time when the so-called New Music of Wagner and Liszt seemed to represent the cutting edge of what was new and exciting in music during the second half of the nineteenth century, Brahms could unfairly be described as something of an anachronism.

Yet his music is innovative in the way in which he almost re-invented Classical models. He also influenced a whole generation of composers as diverse as Dvořák, Elgar, Nielsen and Schoenberg, with the latter acknowledging this in his famous essay 'Brahms the Progressive'. Perhaps, then, this Classical Romantic was the first neo-classical composer, well before that twentieth century vogue was to have such a significant impact.

Tchaikovsky

Peter Tchaikovsky (1840–1893) must surely be one of the most frequently performed composers of all time, and his music is a firm favorite amongst concertgoers. Sadly, with this comes a certain amount of snobbishness; so-called serious musicians have, over the years, dismissed his music as nothing more than pretty tunes and neurotic angst. This perception is far removed from the actual reality, for in this composer we find music which is finely crafted, innovative and which has the spark of genius. Tchaikovsky's melodies are, indeed, often pretty and memorable, but his craft goes much deeper than that. It is also undeniable that his music could be described as burdened with emotional anguish, however that might be defined. Yet it could be argued that Tchaikovsky was so willing to express his neuroses through his music, that it brings out the neurotic bent within listeners.

Very little of Tchaikosvky's chamber and vocal music is regularly performed, and so his reputation today rests largely on his last three symphonies, the *Violin Concerto*, *First Piano Concerto*, the *Romeo and Juliet Overture*, the *Rococo Variations*, the three ballets, the *Marche Slave*, the *Italian Capriccio*, the *Serenade for Strings*, the opera *Eugene Onegin* and, of course, the ubiquitous *1812 Overture*.

Tchaikovsky's gift as a melodist has undeniably helped to maintain his popularity and, over the years, these wonderful melodies have occasionally been adapted and arranged for the more popular musical genres. Their sweeping style and shape have certainly been emulated by Hollywood composers to accompany epic films. In fact, Tchaikovsky's melodic invention is at times breathtaking.

Take one of his most enduring works, the *First Piano Concerto in B flat minor* (1875). It is often forgotten that he composed a further two piano concertos, though the seldom performed *Third* is merely an arrangement for piano and orchestra of a movement from his aborted *Symphony in E flat*. Maybe the neglect of the *Second Piano Concerto in G* has something to do with the sheer memorability of the *B flat minor's* melodies. The *First Piano Concerto's* opening is, along with the opening of Grieg's *Piano Concerto*, perhaps the most unforgettable and oft-whistled of concerto openings. The listener forgets that once this opening has run its course, it is never heard again, and whilst Tchaikovsky spins it out for some time, it is a mere ninety bars in a movement which lasts for almost seven hundred. It has often been criticized because of this: a memorable idea which the composer seems to waste. In fact, it serves the purpose for which it was written, namely as a curtain-raiser for one of the longest and most complex first movements in the regular concerto repertoire.

That the introductory theme never recurs is of little concern to the listener, in a work which is brimming with unforgettable melodic ideas, piano writing which juxtaposes poetry and dazzle, plus sensitive orchestration. Little wonder, then, that the *Second Piano Concerto* has a tough act to follow. Though occasionally performed, its relative neglect has more to do with the *First Piano Concerto's* success, rather than its own inadequacies.

Compared with the last three of Tchaikovsky's symphonies, the first three symphonies are not as regularly performed. Of the last three, the *Fourth Symphony in F minor* (1877), and the *Sixth Symphony in B minor, Pathétique* (1893), are the most innovative. Though the *Fifth Symphony in E minor* (1888) is an established orchestral warhorse, it has not survived without some criticism.

The first three movements are beyond reproach. The motto theme which opens the work is skilfully reworked into the other movements, so that this use of what is known as cyclic form artfully acts as a unifying feature. The third movement becomes one of Tchaikovky's finest orchestral waltzes, and the slow movement, with its breathtakingly haunting horn solo, has an emotional range worthy of Beethoven. Tchaikovsky did himself no favors when he criticized this symphony for its lack of organic cohesion, for such criticism has given others *carte blanche* to add further censure to the composer's. In reality, any weaknesses in this symphony are the domain of the finale. The use of cyclic form helps to unify this movement with the others, and the material is memorable. What the movement lacks, however, is the type of momentum and general unity that one discovers in other large-scale structures found in Tchaikovsky's mature works.

The lack of cohesion identified by the composer surely alludes exclusively to this movement, for it is music which sounds sectional at best, and disjointed at worst. Moreover, the blaring out by trumpets and horns in the final bars of the first movement's principal theme, the trumpets marked *ffff*, has been commented upon as sounding hollow and forced. In a concert setting, however, with Tchaikovsky's wonderful sense of orchestral color, this peroration never fails to win hearty applause. For the audience, it is the overall effect that matters, and not structural shortcomings, and the *Fifth Symphony* has rightly endured as an orchestral favorite.

Like the *Fifth Symphony*, the *Fourth Symphony* also employs a motto theme, a fanfare-like idea heard at the outset, as a unifying feature. Though this was written some ten years before the *Fifth*, Tchaikovsky integrates the motto more imaginatively than in the later symphony. Thus it becomes organically part of the first movement's structure, rather than a bolt-on idea. For example, in this movement, it is employed as part of the transition from exposition to development, from development to recapitulation, from recapitulation to coda. It is heard again in the finale but, in truth, whilst its announcement is undeniably exciting, it does not play the vital structural role that it does in the first movement. Tchaikovsky attempts a greater sense of cohesion in the *Fifth Symphony*, where the motto is heard more prominently in the second, third and fourth movements.

The first movement of the *Fourth Symphony* is not only one of Tchaikovsky's most ambitious and complex, but it is innovative in the way in which he contrasts tonalities. He here dispenses with the Classical relationships between keys – tonic-dominant, and the like – and employs a type of axis tonality whereby the keys move up, instead, in minor thirds. Using this circle of thirds, it allows Tchaikovsky to arrive back at his home key of F minor.

The Baroque and Classical masters used circles of fifths; Vivaldi, for example, made a career from it. But by using circles of thirds on such a large scale, Tchaikovsky is apparently making the statement of relinquishing Classical long-term tonal planning. He is also here challenging the Classical relationship between key and structure, by delaying the final announcement of the home tonic until the coda. This first movement was to teach later composers a great deal in its reinterpretation of the sonata form ideal. Its use of axis tonality, a term used above to describe Tchaikovsky's key progessions in thirds, was to be further exploited, to name one composer, by Bartók.

At the behest of his patron, Madame von Meck, Tchaikovsky supplied a program for his *Fourth Symphony*. The idea sat uneasily with the composer and, unlike, for example, Berlioz, Tchaikovsky's narrative came after the work's completion. He also jotted thoughts for a program for his *Fifth Symphony*, again bound up with the Beethovenian idea, *pace* the latter's *Fifth Symphony*, of the 'fate' motto theme.

In some ways Tchaikovsky was more experimental than Brahms. Brahms consolidated the Classical ideal, whereas Tchaikovsky was more willing to challenge it. Tchaikovsky's influence was also more far reaching than that of Brahms. That Rachmaninov's music should be influenced by Tchaikovsky should not surprise us. But he also played his part in influencing composers as diverse as Puccini and, in particular, Stravinsky, and two composers who represented opposite poles of early twentieth century symphonic thought: Mahler and Sibelius.Indeed, Mahler might have been influenced by the programmatic, and quasi-autobiographical, elements of Tchaikovsky's symphonies.

Concerning what is probably Tchaikovsky's greatest achievement, his *Sixth Symphony*, known as the *Pathétique*, his initial idea was, in fact, for its title to be *Program Symphony*, though without a specific narrative. Even so, well before the work was finished, Tchaikovsky had made a few notes, for his own reference, which allude to some sort of vague program of the symphony's essence being about life, love, disappointment and death. The fact that he died just days after the premiere have led all kinds of commentators to unhelpfully view the work as premonitory. More so than any programmatic elements, what undoubtedly influenced Mahler, and other later symphonists was the innovatory nature of the *Pathétique*.

Unlike the *Fourth* and *Fifth* symphonies, the *Pathétique* does not use a motto theme. Despite this, and even though its first movement is the most clear cut and compressed of the later symphonic sonata form movements, resemblance to Classical tradition ends here. The second movement is a waltz, the last of Tchaikovsky's orchestral waltzes. His music abounds in waltzes, from the *Fourth Symphony's* second subject in the first movement, to the *Fifth Symphony's* third movement, via the grand waltzes in the ballet scores, to name but a few.

The idea of placing a waltz within a symphony was hardly new, as Berlioz had done just that in the *Symphonie Fantastique* more than sixty years earlier. The *Pathétique's* waltz, though, seems to be the apotheosis of all of them, a waltz that cannot be free, and one which is impossible to dance to, for it is in an iambic five beats, rather than three in the bar. Its middle section has a hypnotic effect, for it consists of a floating melody over fifty-six bars (if the repeats are observed) of a pedal D, where this note is repeated in the basses, bassoons and timpani two hundred and thirty-two times.

In some sort of oblique reference to Classical symphonic tradition, this dance movement is followed by what seems like a finale, such is the sense of momentum, climax and tumultuous close achieved by the march-like third movement. Symphonic marches were by then well-worn formulas, and Tchaikovsky might, again, have had his eye on the *March to the Scaffold* from the *Symphonie Fantastique*. In fact, Tchaikovsky's march is a false finale, and it leads into the true finale, not before uninitiated audiences applaud, believing that the work has ended. And here is Tchaikovsky's most daring symphonic innovation, for innovation it truly is. For his finale, he offers an emotionally exhausting slow movement, thereby shifting the emotional weight of the symphony from the middle, where the slow movement normally is, to the end. It influenced a whole generation of works by later composers, from Mahler's slow finales, to those found in Shostakovich's symphonies, to the slow finales of Berg's *Lyric Suite* and Bartók's *Second String Quartet*.

Tchaikovsky's experimentation with large-scale form did not begin and end with the symphonies. Of his other significant orchestral works, the *Fantasy Overture, Romeo and Juliet* demonstrates just what a master of orchestration he was, not least here in the musically pictorial representation of sword fights. The second subject of this ambitious and wonderfully controlled sonata form structure is the famous love theme, described by the composer Rimsky-Korsakov as one of the finest tunes by any Russian. Without a doubt, it is a singularly unforgettable moment when it is first announced, with its full emotional pull not unleashed until its recapitulation towards the end of the work. Such control over his material was not arrived at overnight, and although the work was composed in 1869, it was revised a year later, and then again in 1880.

Of his other concert works, the *1812 Overture* is always a good excuse to bring artillery into the concert hall, though Tchaikovsky had a generally low opinion of the work. It is, on balance, formulaic and bombastic, despite its popularity. Written at the same time, 1880, is the gorgeous *Serenade for Strings in C*. Intimate, beautifully proportioned and sensitively scored, it is a world apart from its noisy contemporary. Such elegance is also found in the charming *Variations on a Rococo Theme* (1876) for cello and orchestra. Two years later, in 1878, Tchaikovsky composed his *Violin Concerto in D*, deservedly one of the most frequently performed of concertos.

There is an amount of Tchaikovsky's orchestral music which is never aired, and sometimes for good reason, for it does not always match the works which are regularly performed. But there are two works in particular which deserve more frequent outings: the *Symphonic Fantasia, Francesca da Rimini* (1876), and the *Manfred Symphony* (1885). Perhaps *Manfred's* neglect has something to do with its length (as it is longer than any of the symphonies), or even its quiet ending, and perhaps *Francesca da Rimini's* neglect has something to do with it being overshadowed by *Romeo and Juliet*. They are unjustly overlooked, and both should take regular places on concert programs. Similarly neglected are the two interesting orchestral Suites of 1883 and 1884.

Finally, a word about the ballets, *Swan Lake* (1876), *The Sleeping Beauty* (1889), and *Nutcracker* (1892). They are the three most popular ballets of all time, achieving the rare accolade of being in every ballet company's repertoire, as well as being frequently performed on the concert platform, though the *Nutcracker* music is the only one that Tchaikovsky actually turned into a concert suite. Such is the quality of music in these scores, and the imaginative orchestral coloring, that the music survives outside its visual environment of the theater. Tchaikovsky elevated the whole concept of fairy-tale ballet, paving the way for the landmark ballet scores of Stravinsky, Prokofiev, Ravel and others.

Dvořák

Championed by his friend Brahms, the music of Antonin Dvořák (1841–1904) is influenced by the older composer. In addition, it is shot through with nationalism, a feature which gained momentum as the nineteenth century progressed. Like Beethoven and Schubert before him, and Mahler and Vaughan Williams who came later, Dvořák completed nine symphonies, in addition to concertos for violin, cello, and piano, plus miscellaneous orchestral works. Had only his last three symphonies and *Cello Concerto* survived, Dvořák would still be remembered as a nineteenth century master, and it is these works which today largely carry his reputation. In addition, he composed *Slavonic Dances* for orchestra, which have become standard encore fodder. They are skilfully crafted, allowing Dvořák free reign to express the nationalist Czech side to his musical personality. If these dances offer suitable 'curtains' for concerts, his well-loved *Carnival Overture* (1891) is one of the most imaginatively and vividly orchestrated of curtain-raisers.

From the *Fifth Symphony in F* (1875) onwards, there is a clear progression in terms of technique and assuredness in Dvořák's handling of symphonic form. The first four symphonies are seldom performed, but the *Fifth Symphony* is certainly the first of his symphonies worthy of regular performance. For concert audiences, though, the *Sixth Symphony in D* (1880) is the earliest of the set which has found lasting favor. It contains a wealth of melodic invention which was also to be a hallmark of all the later symphonies. If parts of it are unashamedly Brahmsian, such as the very opening whose character is reminiscent of the opening of Brahms's symphony in the same key (and same meter), this should be viewed as Dvořák's tribute to, and assimilation of, Brahms, rather than any lack of originality. True, Dvořák's sound-world owed much to Brahms. But he had enough of a strong musical personality and imagination to allow his own genius to shine through, so that those Brahms-like moments we find in Dvořák are really incidental to the greater picture.

Harmonic inflections derived from Slavic folk music can be readily found in Dvořák's symphonic writing, such as the juxtaposition of major and minor, or the modal use of the flattened seventh note in a scale, plus rhythmic features. Yet the *Sixth Symphony* is the only mature symphonic work by Dvořák to overtly make reference to the native music of his country. Here, the third movement is a Furiant, and subtitled as such, with its lively cross-rhythms. Even so, the movement is Classically cast, complete with a contrasting Trio section.

In terms of the development of material and the handling of structure, the *Seventh Symphony in D minor* (1885) is Dvořák's closest answer to the symphonic language of Brahms. It is, by far, the darkest of the mature symphonies, with an austerity rarely found in this composer. It is also his most closely argued symphony, and regarded by many as his greatest work. By contrast, the *Eighth Symphony in G*, completed four years later, concerns itself with light, bright melodic ideas, and relatively simple, yet beautifully calculated, orchestral textures. The contrapuntal, harmonic and structural complexities of the *Seventh Symphony* have all but disappeared, producing a simpler and more rhapsodic offering. Undoubtedly, though, it remains one of the most delicious and well-loved symphonies of the century's closing years.

Dvořák's final symphonic offering is the famous *Symphony No. 9 in E minor, From the New World*. It is almost universally, though incorrectly, known as *The New World Symphony*, and has been one of the most frequently performed orchestral works since its successful New

York premiere in 1893. This is well deserved, and although it lacks the intellectual rigor of the *Seventh Symphony*, it is nonetheless something of a masterpiece.

Dvořák was at that time Director of the New York National Conservatory of Music, and whilst various cases have been made to support the view that the work was influenced by native American music, the opposite is, in fact, the case. True, the first movement's second subject might resemble, in part, *Swing Low, Sweet Chariot*, one's imagination might link some of the other themes with African or Indian melodies, and it seems likely that Dvořák was reading Longfellow's *Hiawatha* whilst composing the second movement.

But as far as Dvořák was concerned, the work was a musical letter home to his friends, a homesick message recalling the melodic shapes and rhythmic contours of his homeland's music, thousands of miles away. An expression of this can be found towards the end of the famous Largo, the second movement. Here, twenty-three bars before the end, the music becomes especially intimate. Dvořák reduces his strings to just ten players, all of whom are muted. The main theme is quietly announced, but after four bars it stops, and the music pauses on a silence. It resumes for another bar, but stops again, and then resumes with just solo violin, viola and cello. One could speculate that these silences represent the composer catching his breath between homesick sobs. Yet however fanciful this might sound, what remains is one of Dvořák's most poetic moments.

This Largo is an oft-played work in its own right, though its popularity runs the risk of hiding its subtleties. The opening, for example, deserves special mention in terms of orchestral balance, which precedes the famous cor anglais solo, a melodic idea idiomatically devised for this dark-hued instrument. Not that there should be any question about Dvořák's prowess as an orchestrator, but this movement alone would dispel any.

The *Violin Concerto in A minor* is contemporaneous with the *Sixth Symphony*, and with it shares a wealth of melodic invention, though at the expense of the type of musical argument found in later works. Despite its charm, it has not established itself in the repertoire as firmly as the Tchaikovsky and Brahms violin concertos, both of them written in 1878 at almost the same time as Dvořák's concerto.

By contrast, the *Cello Concerto in B minor* (1895), much admired by Brahms is, along with Elgar's *Cello Concerto*, arguably the finest example of its genre. Interestingly, great art can sometimes be influenced by lesser creations, and in Dvořák's case, he may have been prompted to write his *Cello Concerto* after hearing, in Brooklyn in 1894, a performance of the *Second Cello Concerto* by the now largely forgotten composer Victor Herbert. Dvořák's last three symphonies place the slow movement at the spiritual heart of these works. The same is true of his *Cello Concerto*, whose slow movement is an unending celebration of song-like melody, a feature also found in the second subjects of the outer movements. It is this song-like lyricism that Dvořák so ably matches to the cello in this work. The solo writing is undeniably masterful, not just in the way Dvořák understands how to write for this instrument, but also in how he matches his musical material so stylistically. Structurally, the work is not significantly different from a Classical concerto, though its sound-world is that of the late nineteenth century. Indeed, it is one of the last of the great Classically-cast concertos. It was also to be Dvořák's last major composition, and is a fitting swansong for a composer who, although not at the forefront of innovation or experimentation, was nevertheless one of the masters of his age.

'The Five' and other Russians

Though western Europe had, by the middle years of the nineteenth century, a rich heritage of music, the same could not be said of Russia. When Tchaikovsky was producing his masterpieces between the 1870s and 1890s, he was composing within a fairly recent Russian tradition. The first important Russian composer whose music is still performed, was Michail Glinka (1804–1857). His well-known overture to his Pushkin-inspired opera *Russlan and Ludmilla* (1842) is one of his few regularly performed works. Glinka was influential in paving the way for music which can be specifically identified as Russian, if only for the aforementioned opera, and his patriotic opera *A Life for the Czar* (1842).

Whilst the names of The Five, or The Mighty Handful, as they are sometimes referred to, are well enough known, a surprisingly small amount of orchestral music by them is regularly performed. The group consisted of Alexander Borodin (1833–1897), César Cui (1835–1918), Mily Balakirev (1837–1910), Modest Mussorgsky (1839–1881), and Nikolai Rimsky-Korsakov (1844–1908). Tchaikovsky was never part of the group, though he was championed at one stage by The Five's leader, Balakirev. The Five grouped themselves in the 1860s with the aim of creating a truly Russian type of music, and it is perhaps little wonder that Tchaikovsky was never part of them, for his music is more Western, and only mildly nationalistic. The music of Cui and Balakirev is now seldom performed, with Balakirev's most well-known piece being *Islamay* for piano.

Performances of Borodin's orchestral music are largely confined to his popular *Second Symphony in B minor* (1876), the overture and *Polovtsian Dances* from his operatic masterpiece *Prince Igor*, started in 1869, but left unfinished at the composer's death, and the short, atmospheric piece *In the Steppes of Central Asia* (1880), dedicated to

Liszt. Mussorgsky's greatest work was his opera *Boris Godunov* (1869), one of the supreme nineteenth century operas. His orchestral output is today known by just the one work, the popular orchestral showpiece *A Night on a Bare Mountain* (1867), though his piano piece *Pictures at an Exhibition* (1874) has found its way into the orchestral repertoire thanks to orchestral arrangements by Ravel and others.

Rimsky-Korsakov's claim to fame was fourfold. Firstly, his orchestral music is the most frequently performed of any by The Five. Secondly, he was one of the finest orchestrators of the nineteenth century.

Thirdly, his influence was perhaps the most significant of The Five. And fourthly, he is remembered as the teacher of that twentieth century giant, Igor Stravinsky. His wonderfully colorful *Capriccio Espagnol* (1887) is a permanent favorite, and the *Russian Easter Festival Overture* (1888) is an occasional visitor to the concert hall, as are some smaller works such as the popular *Flight of the Bumble Bee*, from the opera *The Tale of Czar Sultan* (1900).

Rimsky's best-loved work, however, is the symphonic suite *Scheherazade* (1888), his most ambitious orchestral piece. Originally planned as a programmatic symphony, its subject, borrowed from the well-known Persian folklore tales, *The Arabian Nights,* is whimsical enough to demonstrate his talent for orchestration, and for the sometimes exotic musical language of The Five to inform this eastern tale. *Scheherazade* is one of those hybrid works, neither symphony nor suite, but something in between. Its movements are lengthy enough to place it within a symphonic framework, yet its lack of musical development, in the Classical sense, and reliance instead on varied repetition supported by colorful orchestration, lacks the rigor of symphonic structure, placing it more within the realms of a suite.

Amongst the younger generation of Russians is Alexander Glazunov (1865–1936). A pupil of Rimsky-Korsakov, he went on to become a fine teacher, and is now largely remembered as Shostakovich's mentor. His works, which include eight symphonies, are not frequently performed, though his best known orchestral work is the *Violin Concerto in A minor* (1904).

There were a host of other Russian composers, active at the end of the nineteenth century, and composing well into the twentieth century. They are today largely unknown to concertgoers, but include: Anatol Liadov (1855–1914), who composed several tone poems; Vladimir Rebikov (1866–1920); Nikolai Tcherepnin (1873–1945), who composed a number of ballet scores; Reinhold Glière (1875–1956), whose many works include a concerto rarity – one for harp; Nikolai Medtner (1879–1951), whose emotionally charged piano concertos have never captured the public's favor in the same way as Rachmaninov's; Nikolai Miaskovsky (1881–1950), who composed no fewer than twenty-seven symphonies.

The music of Alexander Scriabin (1872–1915) does not always fit easily with that of his Russian contemporaries. His appearance on concert programs is now usually confined to his solo piano music. On the one hand, the poetic nature of his music can be traced back to Chopin. On the other hand, his more chromatic music is closer to the sound-world of Wagner.

However, it is often forgotten that he was something of an innovator in things harmonic. He was, for example, experimenting with non-triadic harmony based on superimposed fourths, notably demonstrated in his so-called 'mystic chord', which forms the basis of his symphonic work *Prometheus – The Poem of Fire* (1910), scored for piano, orchestra and chorus. Scriabin also envisaged that this work should be performed with a 'color keyboard', designed by the physicist Alexander Moser, which would project colors according to the emotional dictates of the music. This strange-looking contraption is currently housed in Scriabin's Moscow apartment, now a museum. Whether the keyboard was ever used in performance, is doubtful.

Fanciful though Scriabin's idea was, it nevertheless points to his innovative multimedia vision that performance of his music should be harmonized with other non-musical elements, in this case light and color. In fact, Scriabin probably suffered from synaesthesia, where for him sounds actually 'projected', or at least suggested, color. The only other orchestral work which is occasionally performed, is *The Poem of Ecstasy* (1908).

His most ambitious work was never composed, though he cogitated on the idea for at least the last ten years of his life. He referred to it as the *Mystery*, a gigantic multimedia work to be performed in a far-eastern amphitheater, resulting in a spontaneous Nirvana-type state for the tens of thousands who would witness it.

Other nineteenth century Romantics and Nationalists

Composing in an overtly Austro-German style, and obviously influenced by Brahms, rather than Wagner, was the Cologne-born Max Bruch (1838–1920). Though a prolific composer, he is principally remembered today for his deservedly popular *First Violin Concerto in G minor* (1867), though a further two violin concertos, now less frequently performed, followed. The *Scottish Fantasy* (1880), also for violin and orchestra, is amongst Bruch's best known works. Similarly well known, is *Kol Nidre* (1880) for cello and orchestra. *Kol Nidre* is Hebrew for 'All vows', the ancient Jewish prayer and traditional melody chanted on the eve of Yom Kippur, its soulfulness captured in this beautiful setting.

In contrast to the symphonic tradition of the nineteenth century Austro-German composers, there was a lighter and more entertainment-based orchestral style. Johann Strauss the elder (1804–1849) was the founder of the Strauss dynasty. His most popular work is the *Radetzky March* (1848) which, if it does not always appear on the printed program for Viennese evenings, is more often than not offered as an encore. It was this composer who set the seal on a style of richly melodic waltzes, polkas, gallops and marches, though the waltz had been gaining in popularity since the end of the eighteenth century.

His son Johann Strauss II (1822–1899) ensured that Vienna became known as the Waltz City, whilst he was dubbed the Waltz King. He composed countless famous waltzes, including *By the Beautiful Blue Danube* (1867), commonly referred to as *The Blue Danube*, a work much admired by Brahms. Other composers, notably Josef Lanner (1801–1843) and Franz Léhar (1870–1948), contributed to this alluring style.

Of other German composers of the late nineteenth and early twentieth century, the only orchestral work by Karl Goldmark (1830–1915), a composer far more popular in his own lifetime, which was once widely performed, is the *Rustic Wedding Symphony* (1877). Likewise, only a minority of the works by the German composer Max Reger (1873–1916) is orchestral. Writing in what is essentially a post-Brahmsian style, though with a chromatic bent derived from Wagner, and a contrapuntal style harking back to Bach, he is largely championed by organists, and his many works for that instrument often appear on recital programs. His orchestral music, however, has never been part of the regular repertoire with, perhaps, the exception of his *Orchestral Variations on a Theme by Mozart* (1913).

One of the finest of nineteenth century song-writers, the only orchestral work by Hugo Wolf (1860–1903) which is performed, is the delightful *Italian Serenade* for strings, discovered after his death. Though born in Moscow, Hans Pfitzner (1869–1949) was of German parentage, and he spent most of his life in Germany. Chiefly remembered for his opera *Palestrina*, his orchestral works are rarely played, a neglect in part caused by his blatant pro-Nazi stance during World War II. *The Fourth Symphony* (1933) by Franz Schmidt (1874–1939), is the only work of his regularly performed outside his native Austria. The reputation of his compatriot Franz Schreker (1878–1934) now largely rests on his pedagogy, though his charming *Chamber Symphony* (1916) is occasionally performed.

Of later composers, the German Boris Blacher (1903–1975) is mainly remembered for his entertaining *Paganini Variations* (1947), whilst the most significant Austro-German symphonist of that generation is Karl Amadeus Hartmann (1905–1963). He composed eight symphonies, in a style influenced by Berg, Bartók and Hindemith, though they are infrequently performed outside his native Germany.

The orchestral repertoire has few nineteenth century northern European works which are recurrently performed. For most concertgoers, the only significant name is that of the Norwegian Edvard Grieg (1843–1907), though the music of the Danish composer Niels Gade (1817–1890) and Grieg's compatriot Christian Sinding (1856–1941) should not be overlooked. Sweden's most significant nineteenth century orchestral composer was Franz Berwald (1796–1868) who composed six symphonies, though only four are extant. The *Second Symphony, Sinfonie Singulière* (1845), his finest, is occasionally performed, and can certainly stand against contemporary symphonies, such as those by Mendelssohn or Schumann.

Later, the Swedish composer Wilhelm Stenhammar (1871–1927) similarly produced orchestral music of distinction. His early works were influenced by the German Romantics such as Wagner and Bruckner, though he later turned, instead, to the symphonies of Sibelius and Nielsen for his inspiration. His *Second Symphony* (1915) in particular, demonstrates his assured handling of large-scale, rugged symphonic design.

In truth, however, especially in the nineteenth century, Scandinavia was slow in producing great composers and great music. Many of the composers in this region were German educated, and consequently their style betrays their education. In spite of his Leipzig training, Grieg eventually transcended such German influence. By the age of twenty, his fervently nationalistic friend, Richard Nordraak, had introduced him to Norwegian folksong, an influence which was to permeate his music. The assimilation of such national music marked the only stylistic change in his output, because unlike many composers, his music did not necessarily become more refined as he matured. And in spite of a certain amount of European travel, he remained primarily a local composer. That his music spread beyond his native Norway says much about the undeniable flashes of genius that Grieg's music exhibits.

Today, his reputation rests largely on the finely crafted incidental music for Ibsen's *Peer Gynt* (1888), the charming *Holberg Suite* (1884) for strings, the *Norwegian Dances* (orchestrated by Hans Sitt), some of the delightful *Lyric Pieces* for piano, a number of songs, and the *Piano Concerto in A minor* (1868). This is Grieg's only large-scale orchestral work in the regular repertoire. It is one of the most popular of all concertos, and it is easy to understand why: although unquestionably influenced by Schumann's *Piano Concerto*, it brims with memorable and imaginatively developed melodic invention, much of it modelled on the shapes of Norwegian folksong. The piano writing is highly virtuosic – Grieg was a fine pianist himself – the orchestral accompaniment assured and sympathetic, and it is structurally skilfully proportioned. Musical legend tells us that shortly after composition, Grieg showed the score of the new work to Liszt, who sight-read it through at the piano, playing both solo and orchestral parts!

In addition to Dvořák in nineteenth century Bohemia (today part of the Czech Republic), Bedrich Smetana (1824–1884) deserves mention. He is now remembered for his popular operatic masterpiece *The Bartered Bride* (1866) and its well-known, lively overture, plus some fine chamber music. Of his purely orchestral music his cycle of six symphonic poems, *Ma Vlast* (*My Homeland*) are the only ones to be regularly performed. Though to some extent modelled on Liszt's symphonic poems, they are structurally far simpler.

As with so much of Smetana's music, and in common with Dvořák's, it draws much from the syncopated and springy rhythms which permeate Czech folk music. The music is also overtly melodic, memorably so, almost naively descriptive, and orchestrally colorful. There is no finer example of these features than in the second of these symphonic poems, Smetana's most well-known piece, *The Moldau* (or *Vltava*, 1874), the title referring to Prague's river. Its song-like main theme was eventually adapted, and only slightly altered, as Israel's national anthem.

Though not as fervently nationalistic as the Czechs or Scandinavians, the French produced an array of interesting composers in the generation following Berlioz, and they form a link between his startling experimentation, and that of Debussy. The *Symphony in D minor* (1889) by César Franck (1822–1890), is a relatively rare example of a nineteenth century French symphony still in the regular repertoire. Franck's chromatic style owes something to Wagner, though as he was a fine organist, one is not surprised to find Bach-like polyphony in his use of contrapuntal devices such as canon and ground bass. His sometimes dense orchestral textures are also evidence of his organ-loft background. Despite this German influence, there is a fluidity of form and thematic transformation which recalls Berlioz. Though he did not employ the latter's *idée fixe* principle, his use of cyclic form in his *Symphony* demonstrates some traits of the older composer. Franck's *Symphony* is also a good example of telescoped symphonic form, and the middle of the three movements combines slow movement with scherzo. The only other regularly performed orchestral work by Franck is the *Symphonic Variations* (1885) for piano and orchestra.

Another worthy and much loved French symphony of this period, is the *Third Symphony*, the so-called *Organ Symphony* (1886) by Camille Saint-Saëns (1835–1921), and dedicated to the memory of his friend Liszt. Whilst Franck's *Symphony* might sound organ-like at times, Saint-Saëns's offering actually includes a prominent organ part. Like

Franck, Saint-Saëns rethinks Classical symphonic form, for he casts the symphony in two parts, each sub-sectioned to suggest four conventional movements. What Saint-Saëns achieves by doing this, is to allow himself a concise type of symphonic development which dispenses with lengthy repetition, development or recapitulation. Within this form, he also employs a cyclic principle, whereby material from the work's opening is heard later on. Indeed, the *Symphony's* popularity often hides the carefully thought out compositional processes within it.

Of special interest to the listener is, of course, the incorporation of an organ, in addition to Saint-Saëns's already large orchestra, including piano, offering quite an aural spectacle. Saint-Saëns was, in fact, a fine orchestrator, and had a wonderful sense of writing idiomatically for any instrument. For example, any movement from his entertaining *Carnival of the Animals*, will demonstrate this, as will the solo writing in the often underrated one-movement *Cello Concerto in A minor* (1873), the four piano concertos, or the well-known and pictorial symphonic poem *Danse Macabre* (1874).

An earlier French symphony is the one in C by Georges Bizet (1838–1873). A student work, it owes much to standard Classical form and *opera buffa* type melodies. In addition to this, his two suites of music composed for Daudet's play *L'Arlésienne* is the only other orchestral music of Bizet's to be regularly performed. Of course, there are the orchestral suites from that remarkable operatic masterpiece *Carmen* (1875), which offer a happy excuse to bring such wonderful music into the concert hall.

The French composers always had an acute ear for interesting and often dazzling orchestral effects. They were, for example, in the early years of the nineteenth century, including harps in their orchestras, a feature almost non-existent in Austro-German music at the time. It is hardly surprising, then, that the great innovations in orchestral technique in the 1830s should come from the Frenchman Berlioz. It was a tradition carried on by later composers. Mention has already been made of Saint-Saëns's imaginative use of the orchestra. Bizet, for example, was including a saxophone in his *L'Arlésienne* music in 1872.

Other popular French orchestral showpieces include *The Sorcerer's Apprentice* (1897) by Paul Dukas (1865–1935), made famous by Mickey Mouse's portrayal of the apprentice in the Disney film *Fantasia* (1941). Edouard Lalo's (1823–1892) picturesque *Symphonie Espagnol* (1873), and Emmanuel Chabrier's (1841–1894) boisterous orchestral rhapsody *España* are part of a tradition of sorts, where French composers draw upon Spanish music for their inspiration. Also composing symphonic music in the French tradition were Franck's pupils Vincent D'Indy (1851–1931), and Ernest Chausson (1855–1899). Two earlier French composers, Charles Gounod (1818–1893) and Léo Delibes (1836–1891) are largely remembered today for their operatic and vocal works, though they were hugely admired in their own day. Music from Delibes's ballet *Coppélia* (1870), and some orchestral music by Gounod is occasionally included in concerts.

Finally, mainly known for his chamber music and wonderfully gorgeous songs, very little orchestral music by Gabriel Fauré (1845–1924) is performed. What is performed is shot through with the sensitivity that is the main characteristic of this subtle composer. His best-known orchestral piece is his incidental music to Maeterlinck's *Pelléas et Mélisande* (1898). His *Dolly Suite* (1893) for piano duet, though heard in its orchestral form, was not orchestrated by the composer.

CHAPTER 6

—

The Twentieth Century (Part I)

By the closing years of the nineteenth century, a diversity of style had been established, far more than in the previous two hundred years. In the Baroque, Classical and early Romantic periods, composers tended to express themselves in essentially the same language. Thus, Bach and Handel were using the same musical syntax as each other, as were Haydn and Mozart, or Schumann and Mendelssohn, for example. By the end of the nineteenth century, composers as different as Brahms and Fauré, Wagner and Dvořák, or Saint-Saëns and Grieg, were all writing at the same time.

As the nineteenth century progressed, the diatonic system of tonality, so firmly established by the time of the High Baroque, was losing its stranglehold. In truth, when this started to happen is anyone's guess. It could be traced back to the late works of Beethoven in the 1820s, though Wagner's *Tristan and Isolde* (1859) is often cited as the defining moment. In different ways, the eventual breakdown of the major/minor harmonic system was to be a prime mover in the works of Debussy, Schoenberg and their followers.

As the old century gave way to the new, this became even more pronounced when considering that twentieth century composers were experimenting with new ideas and language in the 1890s and early 1900s, as they pioneered various 'isms'. These composers include Debussy, Mahler, Richard Strauss, Sibelius, Schoenberg and, a little later, Stravinsky, Bartók, Ives and others. Whilst they engaged with modernism in their own way, some were content to rely on what was essentially the language of late nineteenth century Romanticism, composers such as Elgar and Rachmaninov.

Pointing up the dynamic nature of artistic development, old genres were re-assessed, so that the symphony, under Schoenberg, gave way to the chamber symphony; the concerto, under Bartók, became the concerto for orchestra; whilst none of these titles, old or new, suited someone as individualistic as Debussy. Others were satisfied to rely upon well-established structures, so that Elgar's symphonies or Rachmaninov's concertos could have been composed a generation earlier. Into this wide-ranging environment, came Debussy, who is often described as the father of twentieth century music.

Debussy

Rather like the Impressionist painters, and the literature of the Symbolist poets who influenced him, so the music of Claude Debussy (1862–1918) hints and suggests, rather than boldly states. Romantic rhetoric is replaced with a more shadowy sense of character and atmospheric dream-like moods; interesting indeed for a composer who, in his early years, fell under the influence of Wagner. There is a clear delineation, then, between the music of this Frenchman, and the music being written by his contemporaries elsewhere in Europe.

A defining moment for Debussy was in 1889 when he attended the Paris Exposition. There, he came across indigenous music from Africa, Asia and, most significantly, Indonesia. Well over a hundred years on, the sound of a gamelan is hardly unusual for us, when daily we encounter sounds from around the globe. For Debussy, though, it was a revelation. Pentatonic and whole-tone scales have been well-worn during the past century, but for Debussy hearing these sounds for the first time, they fired his imagination and directly informed his language.

The aural experience of Debussy's music from the 1890s is, then, far more radical than anything in Schoenberg of around the same time. The latter's sound is a direct result of the progression of a European language, whereas Debussy's palette owes some of its influence to sounds which had their origins on the far side of the world, as well as to the rarefied subtleties of Fauré and Duparc, and the program music of the late nineteenth century Russians.

The first orchestral piece of Debussy which brought him to the public's attention, was the *Prélude à l'Après-midi d'un faune*

(*The Afternoon of a Faune*), completed in 1894. It was written as a prelude to Mallarmé's 1876 poem which describes a sultry afternoon where a highly-sexed faune, half man, half goat, flirts with young nymphs. Understated, yet provocatively sensuous, Mallarmé's text and Debussy's music complement one another, and in fact the poet thought very highly of Debussy's composition.

Daring in musical language, *l'Après-midi d'un faune* was, generally, a success, and appreciated by those who understood its originality. It became even more famous in 1912, when the impresario Sergei Diaghilev's celebrated Paris-based Ballets Russes adapted it as a ballet, and where in its closing moments Vaslav Nijinsky (1889–1950), the greatest dancer of his age, covered himself in the faune's scarf, and made suggestive erotic movements on the Paris stage. Although it was just one of many scandals which followed Nijinsky, it did no harm to Debussy's reputation, and highlighted the erotic nature of the music and the poem which inspired it. When Nijinsky danced the part of the faune shortly afterwards in London, the production was somewhat toned down.

Debussy's lifelong fascination with water, and with the sea in particular, resulted in a number of expressive works. Of the orchestral pieces, the most famous is *La Mer* (*The Sea*), completed in 1905, and one of the century's finest, and most loved, orchestral works. There are three movements: *From Dawn to Midday on the Sea*; *Play of the Waves*; *Dialogue of the Wind and the Sea*. Debussy adds a subtitle on the score: *Three symphonic sketches*.

There is something of a paradox here, for although Debussy offers, at the expense of long sustained melodies, an impressionist-like sketch of the sea, with splashes of color here, and splodges of sound there, the use of the word 'symphonic' suggests something else. In truth, on a deeper level, the work is astonishingly well integrated, far more than the listener might appreciate, or even need to know. More obvious is the use of material from the first movement which finds its way into the third.

Debussy's application of exotic color is much in evidence, especially in his use of harps, percussion and whole-tone scales.

Apart from the movement's titles, *La Mer* is not anecdotal, yet it belongs to a tradition of twentieth century orchestral works about the sea. Roughly contemporaneous with it, Vaughan Williams's *A Sea Symphony* and Delius's *Sea Drift* come to mind. By the twentieth century, with rail travel well established, it was far easier for people who lived many miles from the sea to actually experience it, and so, perhaps unlike those from earlier generations, composers could write their nautical works with some degree of familiarity. Moreover, in Debussy's case, he actually harbored a wish to be a sailor.

Debussy's new musical language went much further than merely using a few exotic sounds from non-western traditions. It compelled him to re-assess all aspects of composition: melody, harmony, rhythm and orchestration. He soon realized that melodies based on pentatonic or whole-tone scales could not be sustained by the established harmonic system. So, block chords moving in parallel motion, hitherto forbidden in classical harmony, soon became an essential part of Debussy's harmonic vocabulary. In terms of orchestral texture, he was among the first to fragment the orchestra, using smaller chamber groupings within the full orchestra.

La Mer was not the first of his orchestral works to reflect this. It is evident in his *Trois Nocturnes* (1899), and is carried through to *Images pour Orchestre* (1912). Debussy used the word Nocturnes to portray, in his own words, "all the different impressions and the special effects of light that the word suggests", and its sound-world is far removed from the piano nocturne of Chopin.

The three works which comprise *Nocturnes* have titles which are fanciful enough – *Nuages* (*Clouds*), *Fêtes* (*Fete*), and *Sirènes* (*Sirens*) – but are meant to be mere starting points or suggestions for the mood of the music. *Fêtes*, the best known of the *Nocturnes*, is one of Debussy's most colorful and flamboyant orchestral pieces. Such color is carried over into the three movements of *Ibéria*, itself one of three sections which constitute *Images pour Orchestre*, the others being *Gigues* and *Rondes de printemps* (*Spring Rounds*). The three separate sections of *Images pour Orchestre* are usually played as individual works in their own right.

The closest we get in Debussy's music to a concerto, is the *Fantasie* for piano and orchestra, penned relatively early on in his career in 1890, though revised in 1909. While owing something to the concerto style of the late nineteenth century, it nonetheless looks forward to his mature works, not least in the use of cyclic procedures, where earlier material reappears. The short *Première Rhapsodie* (1910) for clarinet and orchestra, was written as a test piece for the end-of-year wind examinations at the Paris Conservatoire. Also intended as competition pieces, are the two *Danses* (1904) for harp and strings. These works frame the more substantial orchestral output of Debussy.

But by far the most difficult, and in many ways ambitious, orchestral piece by him, is *Jeux*, written for the Ballets Russes in 1913, and choreographed by Nijinsky. Its scenario was quite unlike any other previous ballet, telling as it does the story of a tennis match in which two women and a man are looking for a lost ball. It explores the *risqué* situation of this *ménage à trois*, within what is one of Debussy's most complex scores. Like so many ballets, it is rarely performed in the theater nowadays, but nor has it won the hearts of concert audiences in quite the same way as his other orchestral works.

Ravel

Maurice Ravel (1875–1937) has the dubious honor of composing what has become one of the most popular orchestral showpieces of all time: *Bolero* (1928). Ravel is the most important impressionist composer after

Debussy, and the popularity of his orchestral music perhaps exceeds that of the latter. In part, this is due to the fact that the standard repertoire contains more orchestral works by Ravel than by Debussy. In part, too, it is because of Ravel's astonishing orchestration, as he was arguably the finest of orchestrators. And also in part it is due to Ravel's clearer sense of melodic line, harmony, textures and forms which are less amorphous than Debussy's. Ravel was more of a classicist than Debussy. Unlike the latter, he accepted the received forms of the classical masters, as in for example, the *Piano Concerto in G*. Ravel himself said that he was more influenced by Fauré, Chabrier and Satie than by Debussy, much though he profoundly admired the latter.

Bolero is a case in point where a simple eighteen-bar melody, and its variant, is repeated over and over again on different instruments. The bolero rhythm on the snare drum persists throughout, and gradually the dynamic range of the piece intensifies right through its fifteen-minute span, from *pianissimo* at its start, to a shattering *fortissimo* tutti climax. The more snobbish of concertgoers might describe *Bolero* as somewhat hackneyed and popularist, but this would be to misunderstand its originality.

To sustain an orchestral piece which is longer than many single symphonic movements using what is essentially one melody, and the same harmonic scheme and key until the closing bars, demonstrates the work of a master composer. Ravel achieves this through careful timing, and subtle orchestration, where his orchestral color changes only gradually, but enough to sustain interest. The use of repetition creates tension and an hypnotic effect which is increased and not released until the C major tonality lurches into a blaze of E major towards the end.

In 1912, ten days after Nijinsky notoriously danced Debussy's *Faune* in Paris, he danced the part of Daphnis in Ravel's new ballet *Daphnis et Chloé*, Ravel's largest orchestral piece. Rarely, if ever, staged in the theater, it is now usually performed in its concert version of two suites. Ravel himself described *Daphnis* as "a choreographic symphony". Whilst no symphony in its shape or plan, it is symphonic in scope, with the same sense of cohesion, and development of material, that one might expect in a symphony, though there is little sense of this when the orchestral suites are performed.

The dawn sequence which opens Scene Three of *Daphnis*, whilst perhaps the most luxurious and wonderfully orchestrated passage in Ravel's output, is even more astonishing in its context of ballet music, compelling the audience to take as much notice of the orchestra pit as the stage itself. This single passage remains a miracle of orchestral technique.

In 1920, Ravel completed *La Valse*. It was first given the title *Wien* (*Vienna*), and with that name was presented to Diaghilev for the Ballets Russes. Diaghilev rejected it, saying that, despite his admiration for it, it was not suited for the ballet. There have been some attempts to mount the work as a ballet, but it remains a concert piece. The original working title gives a clue as to the nature of *La Valse*. It is not a Johann Strauss tribute piece, but it conjures up hazy, fragmented waltzes, making the statement that the era of Johann Strauss and the great Viennese waltz was, by the

1920s, nothing more than a fading memory. Nine years earlier, Ravel had also written a waltz tribute for piano, later orchestrated: *Valses nobles et sentimentales*. At the same time, Richard Strauss was portraying the lost world of the Viennese waltz in his opera *Der Rosenkavalier*, music from which was later made into an orchestral suite.

The four-movement *Rhapsodie espagnole* (1911) is one of a number of pieces where Ravel pays tribute to the country of his mother's birth. His *Ma Mère l'Oye* (*Mother Goose*, 1908) looks further afield, and its occasional reference to the pentatonic scale reminds us that, along with Debussy, Ravel was also present at the 1889 Paris Exposition where he encountered the Indonesian gamelan musicians. *Ma Mére l'Oye* is one of a number of original piano works which were later orchestrated. Others include his suite *Le tombeau de Couperin* (1919), the popular *Pavane pour une infante défunte* (*Pavane for a Dead Infanta*, 1902), and *Tzigane* (1924), originally for violin and piano. Nor did he stop at orchestrating his own piano works. In addition to orchestrating music by Debussy, Satie and others, he also made the famous arrangement of Mussorgsky's *Pictures at an Exhibition*.

Two of Ravel's late works remain amongst his most endearing: the *Piano Concerto in G*, and the *Piano Concerto for Left Hand*, both completed in 1931. This latter work was written for the pianist Paul Wittgenstein (brother of the philosopher Ludwig Wittgenstein) who lost his right arm in the Great War. The *Concerto in G* is as far from the big nineteenth century concerto as one could get. Here is no battle between orchestra and soloist, as in Brahms or Tchaikovsky. Instead, the orchestration is light, the melodic and harmonic inflections often witty and jazzy, its proportions Mozartian. Whilst this concerto is in three movements, and bright in mood, the *Left Hand Concerto* is cast in one continuous movement, though with subsections, and is darker in character.

Despite it being for just one hand, it is highly virtuosic, and listening to it without a score, it certainly sounds as if two hands are at work. The overwhelming originality in this work lies in the fact that there were very few pieces for left hand alone that Ravel could draw upon. Those that he possibly knew, by Brahms, Saint-Saëns and Scriabin, do not go anywhere near the type of inventive virtuosity that Ravel discovered in his *Left Hand Concerto*.

Janáček and other Eastern European Nationalists

Fin de siècle musical style was, as has been explained, something of a fusion, as some composers looked back into the nineteenth century, whilst others forged ahead. It is only since the 1960s that Leos Janáček (1854–1928) has been recognized as the most important Czech composer since Dvořák. His orchestral works are few, and his reputation rests largely on the operas, but also chamber works and two orchestral pieces, the *Sinfonietta* (1927), and the orchestral rhapsody *Taras Bulba* (1918). He lived mostly in the nineteenth century, but is considered a twentieth century composer, as the works which are performed are mainly from that century.

Although initially influenced by Dvořák, Janáček studied Moravian folksong, and his rhythmic motives began, more and more, to take on the speech-rhythms of the Czech language. This had a direct effect on his style, delineated by short repetitive melodic phrases which are themselves based on the rhythmic speech-patterns. Later influenced by Debussy, his harmonic language often includes whole-tone harmonies, adding to a vocabulary which, always firmly tonal, is nonetheless chromatic, modal, and which lends itself to so-called 'added chords' – diatonic chords with added sixths, sevenths and ninths.

All of this is clear to hear in his most popular and finest orchestral work, the *Sinfonietta*. It is, in many ways, Janáček's patriotic tribute to the city of Brno, where he spent most of his life. The opening and closing fanfare music, familiar to many if not by title or composer, was originally written for an alfresco gymnastics festival in 1926. The outdoors nature of the music is underpinned by the great emphasis Janáček places on the wind instruments, whose sound carries far better outdoors than do strings. The brass section alone calls for fourteen trumpets, in addition to what is already a large orchestra. The five movements have descriptive titles: *Fanfares*; *The Castle*; *The Queen's Monastery*; *The Street*; *The Town Hall*.

The orchestral music of Vítězslav Novák (1870–1949) and Josef Suk (1874–1935), both pupils of Dvořák, Suk being Dvořák's son-in-law, have failed to make any lasting impact on the international concert platform apart from, perhaps, Suk's imposing *Asreal Symphony* (1906). However, Bohuslav Martinů (1890–1959) is acknowledged to be the most significant Czech composer in the post-Janáček period, with a large output including at least twenty concertos or concerto-type works, and six symphonies. Considered as Rumania's greatest composer, George Enescu [or Enesco] (1881–1955) penned two popular and colorful *Rumanian Rhapsodies* (1901/1902), the only orchestral works of his which are now regularly played.

Elgar

Although Edward Elgar (1857–1934) lived for the most part in the nine-teenth century, he composed the majority of his music in the twentieth. He is viewed by many as the quintessential Englishman, living mainly in rural England, bestowed with national honors, and becoming Master of the King's Musick. His compositions are also felt to sound English, whatever Englishness in music means.

All of his greatest music was composed between 1899, when he completed his *Variations on an Original Theme*, known as the *Enigma*

Variations, and 1919, the year of the *Cello Concerto in E minor*. Between then and his death, he produced a few short pieces, but no large-scale major works. He left sketches for a *Third Symphony*, commissioned by the BBC, and these have been expanded by the British composer Anthony Payne to make a performing version (1996).

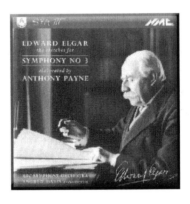

The *Enigma Variations* is a set of fourteen variations, each depicting a friend of the composer, including his wife Alice for the first variation, and himself for the final one. Elgar portrays in music the idiosyncrasies of his friends, occasionally poking gentle fun at them. Scholars have pondered long and hard over the years as to what the original theme is that Elgar based his variations on – hence the title *Enigma*. There have been all manner of fanciful suggestions, ranging from *Auld Lang Syne* and *Rule Britannia*, to the *Dies Irae* plainchant melody and the minuet from Mozart's *Fortieth Symphony*.

But so far, after more than a hundred years, it remains a mystery. The quality of the music within the *Enigma Variations* is beyond question. It demonstrates a composer who has found his voice, writing music which is at once witty and profound. The ninth variation is the famous *Nimrod*. Often played separately, it is not only one of the finest and noblest of pieces, but it provides a fitting swansong to the century of Romanticism.

There is little doubt about the importance of the *Enigma Variations* in the repertoire of British music. From the period after Handel's death until the *Enigma*, British music found little favor abroad. Certainly there was not one single nineteenth century British composer who was equal to the great Europeans of the day. Elgar's legacy is all the more remarkable in the light of a dearth of internationally known works by his British antecedents and contemporaries.

For example, it is difficult nowadays to find live performances of the orchestral works of William Sterndale Bennett (1816–1875), in his own day considered as a home-grown Mendelssohn, and highly regarded by the latter and by Schumann. There was no shortage of nineteenth century British orchestral composers, but to cite Sterndale Bennett as amongst the best-known, perhaps puts the others into obscure perspective. Mention should be made, however, of the Scot Hamish MacCunn (1868–1916), who is remembered today for just one work, the overture *The Land of the Mountain and the Flood* (1889), which is something of a Victorian gem.

Elgar changed Britain's musical reputation, and *Enigma* launched him on a European career. From being a relatively obscure composer and peripatetic music teacher, by 1904 he had received a knighthood. Finally, here was a British composer whose music could stand alongside his contemporaries Mahler and Richard Strauss, the latter and Elgar having mutual admiration for each other.

Elgar was composing in a late nineteenth century, middle European tradition. On the one hand, his music is indebted to Wagner, especially in his orchestration and the use of *leitmotiv* in his oratorios. On the other hand, it closely allies itself with Brahms. Brahms-like melodies, texture, harmonic and rhythmic devices abound. For example, there is a close resemblance between the second subject in the finale of Elgar's *First*

Symphony in A flat (1908), and the corresponding passage in the finale of Brahms's *Third Symphony*. The second main theme in the third movement of Elgar's *Second Symphony in E flat* (1910) could almost have strayed from a Brahms Hungarian dance. Compare, too, the striding opening of Elgar's *Second Symphony* with the opening of Brahms's *Third Symphony* which, as mentioned earlier, was probably influenced by the opening of Schumann's *Rhenish Symphony*, which in turn can trace its roots back to Beethoven's *Eroica*.

Other composers are also apparent in Elgar, and he possibly had an eye on Dvořák's *Cello Concerto* when he composed his *Violin Concerto* (1910). The opening of the concert overture *In the South (Alassio)*, written in 1904, has more than a passing resemblance to the opening of *Don Juan* by Richard Strauss. None of this matters. It does not demonstrate unoriginality on Elgar's part, as countless composers draw on others. Incidentally, the opening of *In the South* is also reminiscent of the opening of Strauss's *Ein Heldenleben*. But this *is* coincidence, as Elgar penned his opening idea as early as 1899, before he heard Strauss's work.

An outstanding feature of Elgar's music is the orchestration, all the more remarkable when we consider that Elgar was largely self-taught. His orchestras tend to use a typically large late nineteenth century scoring. In addition to large orchestral line-ups, the *Cockaigne Overture* (1901) and *Enigma* also employ an ad-lib (ie, optional) organ part in their closing pages. We can also enter Elgar's sound-world of the early twentieth century, for we have numerous recordings of him conducting his own work; early examples of one of the great composers interpreting his own compositions. Some of the orchestral effects in Elgar's works are amongst the most remarkable in the late Romantic repertoire, the closing pages of the *Second Symphony* a case in point. With its shimmering textures, it is what could be described as twilight music, certainly as ravishing as anything in Wagner or Richard Strauss.

The craftsmanship that we find in Elgar, his expert handling of large scale structures – remembering that both symphonies each last for the best part of an hour – and his memorable melodies, from the heartfelt *Nimrod* to the jingoistic *Land of Hope and Glory* (1901), put him amongst the best of his contemporaries. Unlike Mahler and Strauss, however, he was no great innovator. He was content to use the models bequeathed to him, and so his music represents one of the final appearances of nineteenth century Romanticism, rather than a new beginning. His legacy, apart from the wonderful music, was to show British composers that Britain was no longer *Das Land ohne Musik* (The land without music), as it had become known on the continent. Because of Elgar, Britain went on to produce some of the finest of twentieth century composers, and a rich tradition of symphonic writing.

There are, perhaps, a few reasons why Elgar wrote little during the last fifteen years of his life. His wife, Alice, died in 1920, and with her death, something of Elgar died too. She was a source of great encouragement for the composer, and it is debatable that he would have achieved what he did without her. Also, by the time Elgar composed his final orchestral masterpiece, the haunting *Cello Concerto*, there was a new order to things. Stravinsky's *Rite of Spring*, the shocking modernism of Strauss's operas *Salome* and *Elektra*, atonal works of the Second Viennese School, the impressionistic works of Debussy and Ravel, plus the relatively new world of jazz, had hit center stage some years previously. Yet here was Elgar writing in the style of a past generation.

The Great War, too, took its emotional toll on him, and the carnage of that bloodbath was something he found difficult to come to terms with. Even had he lived, it is debatable whether he would have completed his *Third Symphony*. Wonderful though Anthony Payne's realization of Elgar's sketches is, it remains something of an anachronistic sound-world, and maybe Elgar felt this too.

Mahler

Gustav Mahler (1860–1911) is a Janus figure, with one face looking back to his rich nineteenth century Austro-German legacy, the other facing the twentieth century. When he was born, Brahms had not yet written any symphonies, and the ink had hardly dried on the score of Wagner's *Tristan*. At his death, the Great War was less than three years away, the *Titanic* five months from disaster, and Stravinsky had begun to compose for the Ballets Russes. Mahler's Vienna was Europe's powerhouse of Jewish intellectualism, despite its rabid anti-Semitism, with fellow Jews such as Sigmund Freud, Theodor Herzl, Ludwig Wittgenstein, Stefan Zweig, Hugo von Hofmannsthal, and Arthur Schnitzler.

Four of Mahler's symphonies were composed in the nineteenth century, and he was acutely aware of the responsibility of his role as a symphonist, continuing a tradition stretching back to Haydn and beyond. For Mahler, Beethoven was the key to all of this, and Mahler's vision of the symphony is not dissimilar to the one we find in Beethoven's *Ninth Symphony*, the *Choral.*Beethoven's use of voices in this symphony goes further than mere gimmickry. He sees the symphony as essentially a public piece, as opposed to the more private world of chamber music, emphasizing this by including the sound of human voices singing an idealistic hymn of universal solidarity. He even includes in this symphony the sound of a marching band, the type of music that, at that time, normally did not find its way into the concert hall. The point is, he is willing to risk all symphonic convention in order to convey his aspirations through Schiller's message.

Mahler famously said, in conversation with Sibelius, that "a symphony must be like the world – it must contain everything". He accomplishes this, though only achieves it by appreciating that he must be part of the historical dynamic thrust of Beethoven's foresight. In a sense, then, he succeeds in making Beethoven's vision relevant for a late nineteenth century Austrian symphonist, and puts into stark relief Bruckner's symphonies. The latter attempted something similar, though it could be argued that he ultimately fails, noble failure though it is.

Mahler's output is relatively small, mainly consisting of songs and symphonies. There is a marriage between the two, between the Austro-German *Lied* of Schubert, Schumann and Wolf, and the Beethoven symphony. Four of his ten symphonies are vocal, (numbers two, three, four and eight). There is also *The Song of the Earth* (*Das Lied von der Erde*), something of a hybrid between a song cycle and symphony as though, by 1909 when he completed it, this distinction hardly mattered to him.

The vocal symphonies two to four are often referred to as the *Wunderhorn* symphonies, as they use texts from *Des Knaben Wunderhorn* (*Youth's Magic Horn*), an anthology of German folk poetry. Symphonies *Five* to *Seven* are instrumental, and are referred to as the *Rückert* symphonies, as they draw on material from Mahler's settings of poems by Friedrich Rückert. Some of these songs became known as *Kindertotenlieder* (*Songs About the Death of Children*), completed in 1904.

Here we find coming into play, another aspect of Mahler's symphonies: his use of autobiography. It should come as no surprise that autobiographical elements play a role in his music, as it ties in with his assertion that "a symphony must be like the world – it must contain everything". Referencing *Kindertotenlieder* with the symphonies is particularly poignant. Rückert lost a child called Ernst. When Mahler was fourteen, his younger brother Ernst died, and this affected Mahler deeply. Through his music, he tried to exorcize his pain. Yet, in 1907, his own four year old daughter, Maria ('Putzi'), died. Shortly afterwards, Mahler's heart condition, which was to prove fatal, though curable nowadays, was diagnosed. The tragic, at times gloomy, *Sixth Symphony in A minor* (1905) seemed to Mahler, in retrospect, something of a harbinger of catastrophe.

In its finale, he originally included three mighty hammer blows, "blows of fate", as Mahler described them, literally achieved by smashing a mallet onto a block of wood. He had already suffered two calamities in 1907, and out of superstition, and not wanting to tempt fate, he subsequently removed the third of these hammer blows.

For Mahler, life's experience and his music were one and the same thing. Fatalistic to the end, he was nervous about composing his *Ninth Symphony in D* (1910), knowing that Beethoven, Bruckner and Dvořák had not reached beyond that number. And it was, then, a cruel twist of fate, as Mahler would have seen it, that although he started his *Tenth Symphony in F sharp*, he never completed it. Today, it is usually played in Deryck Cooke's performing version (1964).

To underline the sense of autobiography in Mahler's symphonies, one can engage in some calculated speculation. The original version of the *First Symphony in D* (1884, revised 1893, 1896 and 1898), had a program, and a title – *Titan* – both subsequently withdrawn. But the starting point for the funeral march third movement was, according to Mahler, Callot's painting *The Huntsman's Funeral*, where forest animals carry the huntsman's coffin. Its main melody is a minor key version of the well-known round, *Frère Jacques*, perhaps pointing to the child-like starting point of Callot's painting. Apparently, too, it was a song often sung to him by his nanny. After this melody has run its course, what many take to be the music of a marching band is heard. Again, as a child, Mahler lived close to the military barracks at Iglau, and marching bands were frequently seen on the streets a hundred or more years ago.

This all supports Mahler's "a symphony must be like the world" aesthetic; he is including the sounds with which he is familiar. Even so, there might be another explanation, which takes into account the devastating impact that his brother Ernst's death had on him. Ernst was twelve when he died. In Jewish law, he had not therefore reached the important milestone of his thirteenth birthday, his *Barmitzvah*. The funeral march could, in fact, be for Ernst, his *frère*. The marching band sounds far more like a *Klezmer* band, the type of ad hoc ensemble that was an ubiquitous fixture at Jewish wedding and *Barmitzvah* celebrations in central and eastern European communities before they were destroyed by the Nazis.

With its minor key inflection, and intervals of augmented seconds, this music sounds as if it had stepped out of a scene from *Fiddler on the Roof*, rather than an Austrian barrack. It could be dance music for the *Barmitzvah* that never happened. Mahler came from a traditional Jewish background. As a child, he attended synagogue and religious studies, and would have been familiar with *Klezmer* music, and the Jewish secular folk-music of middle Europe. Moreover, the *First Symphony* predates his conversion to Catholicism which, in any case, was a pragmatic move to secure him employment, and he never became a practicing Christian.

Mahler's vision, then, was informed musically by Beethoven and the great Viennese masters, plus Wagner. He was also, interestingly, influenced by Tchaikovsky. We know that Mahler conducted *Eugene Onegin*, giving the German premiere in 1892, and he will have known at least some of Tchaikovsky's orchestral music. Tchaikovksy's innovative use of a slow finale in his *Pathétique Symphony* led Mahler into using a similar device for the finales of his *Third, Ninth* and *Tenth* symphonies. The opening bars of the *Ninth Symphony's* finale paraphrases, even if only subconsciously, the bassoon passage heard immediately before the second subject in the *Pathétique Symphony's* finale. In truth, Tchaikovsky's symphonic structures are terser than Mahler's, which run the whole gamut of human emotion even before the finales are reached.

However, in many ways, a slow, intense and emotionally charged finale in a Mahler symphony is a challenge to a composer who has already written an hour or more of music, because the expressive force has to be maintained. That Mahler sustains his symphonic arguments for rarely less than an hour, and often more, is testament to the quality of his material, and his talent in developing it.

For Mahler, a symphony was a dynamic entity, taking the listener on a journey, progressing towards a goal. Little surprise, then, that he employed what is known as progressive tonality, where a piece, or movement, ends in a different key from where it began. This device, though not new, was refined under Mahler. His harmonic language owes much to the post-Wagnerian Austro-German language, in common with Richard Strauss and Schoenberg though, unlike the latter, he never dispensed with tonality. Even so, his style can be highly chromatic, with sometimes only a vague sense of a clear key, interspersed with occasional passages of direct and simple diatonicism. Structurally, Mahler's huge canvasses mean that symphonies with more than four movements become something of a necessity. He never, though, loses sight of the Classical tradition, and despite the vast scale, he still employs sonata form principles, rondo and variation forms.

Apart from the length of his symphonies, audiences cannot but help notice his striking orchestration. Mahler earned a living as a conductor, usually only managing to compose 'out of season' during the summer. He had, then, firsthand knowledge of the workings of the orchestra which, by the end of the nineteenth century, was an efficient, and at times very large, machine. In fact, it was a period when composers, it seems, were trying to outdo one another in the size of orchestra they wrote for.

The smallest forces Mahler uses in the symphonies appears in the *Fourth*, his shortest. As for the rest, the orchestras are huge, not to mention those places where choirs and solo singers are employed. For example, the *Eighth Symphony in E flat* (1907), is often known as *Symphony of a Thousand*, its forces, though not actually reaching a thousand, being particularly massive.

Even so, whether in this symphony or elsewhere, full forces are used only for effect, with large tracts taken over for chamber-like, transparent textures. The inclusion of guitar and mandolin in the *Seventh Symphony in B minor* (1905), cowbells in the *Sixth*, and sleighbells in the *Fourth*, are employed in those places where delicacy becomes the watchword. In the *Fifth Symphony in C sharp minor* (1902), the orchestra is dramatically reduced to just strings and harp in the famous *Adagietto*, one of Mahler's most remarkably poignant movements, which was rocketed to fame when it was used for the soundtrack of Visconti's 1971 film *Death in Venice*.

Largely unappreciated in his own lifetime, performances of Mahler's music remained few and far between until around the 1960s when he was re-evaluated, not least due to the efforts of the conductor and composer Leonard Bernstein. The only justification for such neglect is possibly due to the difficulties of Mahler's scores, and the practicalities of his large forces. Today, this immensely popular composer is recognized as one of the seminal *fin de siècle* composers.

Richard Strauss

Not unlike Mahler, Richard Strauss (1864–1949) was something of a pioneer, forever redefining the post-Wagnerian Austro-German tradition. Like Mahler, he composed for huge orchestras, and his output is similarly punctuated by much vocal music. Unlike Mahler, though, Strauss was prolific, with most of the tone poems and operas, plus the concertos for horn and oboe, *Metamorphosen* for strings, the orchestral suites from *Der Rosenkavalier*, various other orchestral music, and countless songs, in the regular repertoire.

The concept of the tone poem was not, of course, new by the time he came to compose the first of them, *Aus Italien* (1886). Liszt's symphonic poems, the programmatic symphonies of Berlioz and, before that, Beethoven's *Pastoral Symphony* offered Strauss a rich store of antecedents. *Aus Italien* is more program symphony than single-movement tone poem, though his first single-movement work in this genre closely followed in 1888 with *Macbeth*. Both these works are not as frequently performed as the later and popular tone poems, starting with *Don Juan* (1888), and following with *Tod und Verklärung* (*Death and Transfiguration*, 1889), *Till Eulenspiegels lustige Streiche* (*Till Eulenspiegel's Merry Pranks*, 1895), *Also sprach Zarathustra* (*Thus Spake Zarathustra*, 1896), *Don Quixote* (1897), *Ein Heldenleben* (*A Hero's Life*, 1898), *Symphonia Domestica* (1903), and *Eine Alpensinfonie* (*An Alpine Symphony*, 1915).

Amongst Strauss's early compositions were two symphonies, now rarely played. It is interesting to note that he soon discarded symphonic form for the tone poem, despite the early influence of Brahms. Even the *Symphonia Domestica* and *Eine Alpensinfonie* are tone poems in all but name. After 1915, he relinquished the tone poem entirely, mainly in favor of opera. In the tone poems, there is a shift of emphasis from the relatively short ones up to and including *Till Eulenspiegel*, and the far longer, later ones from *Also sprach Zarathustra*.

Duration aside, all these works use large orchestras, as was so typical of the time. Within the set is a broad canvas of subject matter, from the amorous exploits of *Don Juan*, to the light-hearted medieval pranks of *Till Eulenspiegel*, by way of the then fashionable, though now rather ponderous, philosophizing of Nietzsche in *Also sprach Zarathustra*, to autobiography in *Symphonia Domestica* and *Ein Heldenleben*.

Also sprach Zarathustra had a profound effect on many young composers of the day. After hearing it in 1900, Bartók was inspired to become a composer, and it is not difficult to understand why. Its sound-world is as daring as anything in late Romantic Austro-German music, Mahler included. The audacious and gripping opening, conjuring up something of the brave new world of Nietzsche's epic prose poem, still resonated in the 1960s when it was used as the theme tune for Kubrick's 1968 cult film *2001: A Space Odyssey*.

Strauss did not find it necessary to vocalize Nietzsche; he felt he could portray the sentiments using only instruments. But he was not alone in identifying with Nietzsche's aspirational writings. Mahler had set part of the same poem in his *Third Symphony*, completed in the same year as Strauss's work, and Delius used it in his *Mass of Life* (1905). It has been said that Strauss was no intellectual, and the profound concepts of Nietzsche are somewhat at odds with the rather more mundane subjects of most of the other tone poems.

It is interesting, here, to compare Strauss with Mahler. The latter's take on things philosophical was ideally suited to the weightiness of Nietzsche, the delicate poignancy of the Chinese verse in *The Song of the Earth*, or Rückert's poetry in *Kindertotenlieder*. His use of autobiography is referenced, though just hinted at. Strauss, however, felt thoroughly at home with the bold colors of Nikolaus Lenau's seductive Don Juan story, the comedy of *Till Eulenspiegel*, the forthright autobiography of *Ein Heldenleben* and the domestic (dis)harmony of *Symphonia Domestica*.

Strauss's highly chromatic musical language was a product of its late nineteenth century Austro-German style. It did not go as far as Schoenberg's atonalism, but at times came close to it, not least in the two operas *Salome* (1905) and *Elektra* (1908). Strauss's orchestration, too, reflects its geography and time. It is something of an amalgam of Wagner and Bruckner, with the brilliance and weightiness of the former, plus the latter's use of huge, monolithic blocks of sound. Chamber groupings within the large orchestra are something more particular to Mahler than to Strauss. Even so, there are numerous delicate moments within the tone poems, including the quixotic violin concerto-like portrayal of the composer's wife in *Ein Heldenleben*.

There are also places which are innovatory and stunningly effective, as in the depiction of bleating sheep, cunningly achieved by means of flutter-tongued brass, in *Don Quixote*. Strauss also handles chamber groups with wonderful skill and sensitivity, such as in the Mozartean-like orchestration of the *Oboe Concerto* (1945, revised 1948).

Strauss had a long and productive life. When he was born, Wagner was still composing, and Brahms had yet to complete his *First Symphony*. The Austro-German tradition continued its stranglehold on things musical, and Vienna was currently considered to be the world's musical capital. At his death, Germany was in tatters, following the defeat of history's most evil regime, and the artistic glory of Vienna was but a memory. Strauss was, in truth, the last of the great Romantics, still composing in the late 1940s in an overtly late nineteenth century style. These achingly beautiful and lyrical late works do not hide the daringness of works written some forty or more years earlier. Rather, they have the poignancy, resignation and mellowness of a creative life spanning some sixty years.

Sibelius

Along with Mahler, Jean Sibelius (1865–1957) is the greatest of the *fin de siècle* symphonists, and comparisons between them are almost inevitable. However, at first glance, it might seem that they have little in common: Mahler's symphonies have an average duration in excess of seventy minutes, whereas Sibelius's average out at around thirty-five; Mahler's orchestras are, on the whole, huge, whereas Sibelius's are modest by comparison; Mahler composed vocal symphonies, whereas Sibelius's are purely instrumental; Mahler's symphonies occasionally have an autobiographical sub-text, whereas Sibelius's do not; Mahler devoted all of his creative life to symphonies, whereas Sibelius retired, almost completely, from composition during the last thirty years of his life; Mahler lived in the thriving musical capital of what was Vienna, whereas Sibelius lived in the relative northern European isolation of Finland.

What they do have in common, though, is that they both viewed the symphony as their ideal vehicle for artistic expression. Both considered the genre to be appropriate to their age, and both, in their own way, were hugely indebted to Beethoven, striving to make the latter's symphonic vision relevant to their own period. We have already observed how Mahler achieved this. For Sibelius, he was not preoccupied with Beethoven's public statement of aspirational brotherhood, as expressed in the *Choral Symphony*, which led to Mahler's proclamation, in a conversation with Sibelius, that "a symphony must be like the world". Rather, Sibelius was engrossed with Beethoven's skill at creating symphonic canvases from just a handful of notes, and of diversifying small melodic and rhythmic cells, "profound logic", as Sibelius himself described it. Mahler and Sibelius were, in effect then, two sides of the same symphonic coin, and their joint legacy is that their works form the backbone of twentieth century symphonic thought.

Sibelius composed a fair amount of program music, from the ever-popular early works of *Finlandia* (1899, revised 1900), *The Swan of Tuonela* (1893, revised 1897 and 1900), *En Saga* (1892) and the *Karelia Suite* (1893), to the brooding later tone-poem *Tapiola* (1926). Influenced by the Finnish folk-sagas of the *Kalevala*, his music can conjure up nationalistic fervor on the one hand, such as in *Finlandia*, and, on the other hand, the cold and spectacular tundra of Finland. This latter facet is perhaps more anecdotal than anything else, though for better or for worse, his music has been described, though in no derogatory manner, as icy, wintry and dark. Sibelius himself commented that he offered pure spring water, rather than cocktails.

Popular though the works mentioned above are, and to these we should also add the *Violin Concerto in D minor* (1903, revised 1905), Sibelius's most innovative works are the seven symphonies, plus *Tapiola*. The *First Symphony in E minor* (1899), and *Second Symphony in D* (1902), are the most conventional of the set. The *First* employs Sibelius's largest symphonic orchestra, though still modestly sized when compared with Mahler. Certainly, the orchestral color of this work owes something to the Russians, as do the harmonic and melodic inflections. Structurally, the work breaks no new ground, yet its bleak slow opening and its subsequent dramatic main theme, is a harbinger of what was to follow in the later works. With the *Second Symphony*, Sibelius has moved on and, symphonically, is beginning to experiment with the profound logic and unity of design which was to become the innovative mark of his later compositions. This work remains one of the most frequently performed of twentieth century symphonies.

The *Third Symphony in C* (1907) is something of a watershed in Sibelius's output. Though not quite his shortest, at around twenty-five minutes, and in three movements, it demonstrates just how far Sibelius had traveled in the five years since his previous symphony. The rhapsodic elements in the earlier symphonies are now replaced by terse melodic and rhythmic cells which grow organically.

The opening's use of a simple, almost Haydnesque, diatonic figure, with much repetition, and comprised entirely of quavers and semiquavers, is treated in much the same way that Beethoven uses similar ideas. It is as though Sibelius has stripped away one hundred years of Romantic rhetoric in favor of Classical line. This type of neo-classicism predates Stravinsky's or Prokofiev's by some fifteen years, and is Sibelius's innovative response to tonality and symphonic form at a time when Debussy and Schoenberg were forging ahead with their new musical syntax.

The *Fourth Symphony in A minor* (1911) reverts to a four-movement scheme. The musical argument throughout is sustained by the unifying feature of the interval of a tritone, in this case the notes C to F# heard melodically at the outset. The tritone is an unstable interval, traditionally used with caution, and herein lies the paradox. Sibelius uses it to unify. But he also uses it to accentuate melodic, harmonic and tonal tension, in much the same way that Classical composers relied on the tensions and relaxations between closely related keys in sonata form structures. So although Sibelius's compositional aspiration is Classical, aurally there is nothing Classical about it.

The *Fourth Symphony* was Sibelius's most tautly argued work to date, and he originally felt that its successor, the *Fifth Symphony in E flat* (1915, revised 1916 and 1919) would similarly work in four movements. In its final form, however, Sibelius, now forever seeking structural contraction, telescoped the four movements into three, with the middle movement a Classically poised set of variations to act as a foil to the weighty arguments of the outer movements.

The first movement is an excellent example of how Sibelius achieves symphonic growth, for it begins quietly with a slow and drawn-out horn-call. Ten minutes later, the orchestra is going at full pelt, with rapid, loud music. The listener is unaware of how, and when, Sibelius changes gear, of how this magical opening leads into a blazing peroration. This technique, of Sibelius playing tricks with the listener's aural perception, is taken a stage further in the finale. Its opening is a scurrying idea with some nervous energy. There soon emerges, however, another horn-call idea. The *Symphony's* opening misty and tentative horn-call, now becomes, in the finale, something more harmonically and rhythmically static, confident in character. Here, Sibelius's trick is to reach an accommodation, not a bold contrast, between the scurrying music, and the self-assured horn music.

To all intents and purposes, Sibelius had by now put down all the markers for his most controversial and daring work, his final symphony. But not before his reversion, again, to a four-movement structure in the *Sixth Symphony in D minor* (1923), which is perhaps the most enigmatic of the set. Listeners seeking broad melodic ideas and spectacular orchestral effects will find this symphony the least able to offer these. What there is in abundance, however, is restraint and reflective austerity.

There is something of this also in the *Seventh Symphony in C* (1924), though there is also boldness aplenty in what is, in effect, Sibelius's most audacious work. It is in one continuous movement, and lasts barely twenty minutes. Its original working title was *Fantasia Sinfonica*, as though Sibelius himself was unsure as to the precise nature of the work. Since the 1920s, musicologists have argued copiously over whether it is, in fact, in one continuous movement, whether there are elements of separate movements, whether Sibelius uses a type of sonata form or rondo form. In the event, this nomenclature is unhelpful in such an astoundingly original work. All that can be said with any certainty, is that the *Seventh Symphony* is in its own form, that Sibelius had long since broken free from the shackles of sonata form, that the organic organization and temporal tricks that he had been honing, are all resplendent here. It is a work which is the antithesis of Mahler's symphonic model, a work where symphonic argument is telescoped and concentrated, where every note and gesture matters.

In a sense, Sibelius had composed himself into a corner. His creative quest was to contract symphonic form to such an extent, that it was almost re-invented. He demonstrated that it was, indeed, a dynamic genre. How to follow it was the question. And the answer was that he could not. There is evidence to suggest that an eighth symphony, or at least part of one, existed, but was destroyed. With the Seventh, Sibelius said all that he could say symphonically. *Tapiola* followed two years later, by way of incidental music to Shakespeare's *The Tempest*, in 1925. There were a handful of chamber and vocal works but, in the now modernist world of atonality, Stravinsky, Bartók and others, Sibelius remained almost silent right up to his death, a rare example of a composer retiring.

Nielsen

The symphonies of Mahler and Sibelius, and the orchestral works of Richard Strauss have, in terms of popularity, far exceeded the orchestral works of the Danish composer Carl Nielsen (1865–1931). There have been many conductors, composers and other musicians who have championed in particular the symphonies of Nielsen, putting forward the case that these works should stand alongside those by Mahler and Sibelius. In truth, audiences have not taken Nielsen to their hearts in the same way that they have with these other composers.

There is something of a mystery here, for in terms of quality, Nielsen produced some remarkable music. Perhaps audiences have felt that there is nothing in the Nielsen symphonies that quite matches the spine-tingling effect of the first blaze of D major which greets the finale's opening in Sibelius's *Second Symphony*, or the swinging horn theme in the *Fifth Symphony's* finale. They might also feel that Mahler's epic sweep, or Strauss's impressive orchestration have no equivalences in Nielsen. They might also believe that Nielsen's earlier symphonies are too Brahmsian, and that there is a general lack of the type of symphonic experimentation found in Mahler and Sibelius. But styles change, and there is a growing international realization of Nielsen's genius. In any case, one should not forget that until the 1960s, performances of Mahler were few and far between.

Nielsen's style is not easily categorized or defined, straddling as it does a late Romantic and pre-Modernist tradition. His experimentation is not easily identified by the passive listener, but more by the musician. This is largely in the realm of progressive tonality, a device already encountered in Mahler. In Nielsen's *Fifth Symphony* (1922), considered by many to be his finest, the tonality progresses from F to E flat, with the second movement (ie, the structural halfway point), starting on a tonality of B which, tonally, is as far from F as one can get. As early as the *Second Symphony, The Four Temperaments* (1902), there is a progression from the work's opening tonality of B minor, to its concluding one of A major. The *Third Symphony, Sinfonia Espansiva* (1911) is an overtly optimistic work, plain to hear from its very opening.

What followed, the *Fourth Symphony, The Inextinguishable* (1916), with its character of emotional and musical conflict, is rather different, and contains some of Nielsen's most violent music. In a sense, it acts as a type of preparatory exercise for the *Fifth Symphony*, for here, too, there is struggle and conflict. The expansive symphonic arguments that Nielsen had by now perfected, seem to retreat for his *Sixth* and final symphony, *Sinfonia Semplice* (1925), a somewhat enigmatic and understated end to his symphonic career.

Rachmaninov

In common with Elgar, Sergei Rachmaninov (1873–1943) relied on the Romantic musical language and genres of the nineteenth century, even though his creative life went into the 1940s. His poignant and at times brooding language was in some ways an inherent part of his Russian lineage, not least derived from Tchaikovsky who heavily influenced him. Along with Elgar, but unlike Mahler or Strauss, Rachmaninov was no great innovator, his influence limited, and his reputation rests largely on his wonderful gift for memorable melody, dazzling piano writing and effective orchestration. He composed a considerable amount of solo piano music, much of it frequently performed, chamber pieces, songs and stage works.

Of his orchestral output, the *Second Piano Concerto in C minor* (1901), *Third Piano Concerto in D minor* (1909), the *Second Symphony in E minor* (1907), and the *Rhapsody on a Theme of Paganini* for piano and orchestra (1934) are enormously popular. Making increasing concert appearances is a work which is perhaps his fourth symphony in all but name, the *Symphonic Dances* (1940). There are occasional performances of the choral symphony *The Bells* (1913), and the symphonic poem *The Isle of the Dead* (1909).

The story surrounding the composition of the *Second Piano Concerto* is oft-told. Following the ruinous premiere of the *First*

Symphony, Rachmaninov suffered writer's block, and the composer was persuaded to seek hypnotherapy treatment from Dr. Nikolai Dahl. Thanks to Dahl, Rachmaninov began to compose once more, the main result being the deservedly much loved *C minor Concerto*, which carries a dedication to Dahl.

The work's popularity is largely due to the proliferation of memorable melodies. Structurally, this concerto is conventional, although there are some noteworthy features. Firstly, the opening, with its deeply resonant chords, is particularly original. Having the soloist open a concerto had, by 1901, a century-old pedigree. But few concerto openings capture the sense of mystery, suspense and tension that Rachmaninov achieves. Secondly, it begins not in C minor, but F minor, and the music is pulled around into C minor as it works through an extended crescendo. In the same movement, the piano part is almost like a Baroque continuo, much of the melodic interest being in the orchestra, rather than with the soloist.

So large scale are the *Third Piano Concerto* and *Second Symphony*, that it was not unusual at one time for these works to be performed in abridged versions, sanctioned by the composer. This was not so that they would fit on shellac gramophone records, as is sometimes thought, but because they were considered to be overlong and ponderous, a view which seems somewhat astonishing now. The *Third Piano Concerto* is still considered something of an endurance test for pianists, and is amongst the most technically demanding piano concertos in the regular repertoire.

The *Rhapsody on a Theme of Paganini*, one virtuoso paying tribute to another, is also one of those amazingly popular Rachmaninov works. Here is a pianistic and orchestral, and highly concentrated – running at around twenty minutes – *tour de force* of twenty-four variations on Paganini's *Caprice in A minor* for solo violin. Rachmaninov's masterpiece is one of a number of works by various composers, including Brahms, Liszt and Lutosławski, based on this piece by Paganini. Complex themes rarely lend themselves well to variation, and Paganini's theme is simple enough, with its repeated rhythmic motive, and melodic and harmonic sequences, allowing for development and diversification. Often appearing on popular classical music compilations as a stand-alone item, the eighteenth variation is one of Rachmaninov's most memorable moments. A familiar Rachmaninov sound-world, it concerns itself with typical lush Romanticism. This, though, belies its invention, for this variation is an upside down version, an inversion, of the semiquaver tag in Paganini's theme.

Of the other large scale works, the *First Piano Concerto in F sharp minor* (1891, revised 1917), is not as frequently performed as the *Second* and *Third* concertos, despite its later revision, and its neglect is regrettable. Rachmaninov was barely eighteen when he completed this work, yet even at this early stage, it demonstrates his skill at writing piano music which, although highly virtuosic, nonetheless has musical substance. The first movement especially, with its opening soaring melody, looks ahead to those unforgettable themes in the *Second* and *Third* concertos and the *Second Symphony*. The short second movement is as delicate and beautifully balanced as any corresponding movement in later works. The *Fourth Piano Concerto in G minor* (1926, revised

1927 and 1941) has, since a poorly received premiere, never won the hearts of pianists or audiences. In this case, it may be due to a level of thematic and structural sophistication and conciseness that one does not necessarily find in the earlier works, plus melodic ideas which are, in the main, unexceptional.

With the symphonies, the *First in D minor* (1895, revised 1896), received a disastrous reception at what was a deficient premiere performance conducted by Glazunov who, allegedly, was drunk at the time. Largely forgotten until the 1970s, it has since enjoyed something of a revival, though never gaining the popularity of the *Second Symphony*. In the *First Symphony*, as he was later to do in the *Second*, motivic and cyclic form are employed, whereby the opening idea is reworked to produce additional material throughout all the movements. If the *First Symphony* sounds decidedly 'Russian', it is in no small part due to the use of melodic fragments derived from Russian Orthodox chants. Similar ideas, not least the use of the *Dies Irae* chant, are used extensively by Rachmaninov, notably in the *Third Symphony*, *Symphonic Dances* and the *Rhapsody on a Theme of Paganini*.

There is some striking music in the *First Symphony*. Its maturity of style belies the fact that the composer was only in his early twenties, and shows an incremental maturation of style since the *First Piano Concerto*. The finale, in particular, breaks free of overt reference to music of The Mighty Five, or Tchaikovsky, for that matter, and the opening of this movement is as arresting and original as anything being written by Rachmaninov's Russian contemporaries. To be sure, there are structural and orchestral weaknesses with this work. But in design and daringness, it is a far superior work than, say, Borodin's *Second Symphony*, which enjoys more popularity.

The shortest of the symphonies, the *Third in A minor* (1936, revised 1938), is in three movements, though with a middle slow movement which also incorporates a scherzo-like central section. Audacious though the

First Symphony is, epic and rhapsodic though the *Second* is, the *Third* is both more intimate and succinct, very different from the popular *Second*, and this may account for audiences' comparative indifference to it. True, the first movement's second subject, and the middle movement's main theme, are as lyrical as anything in the earlier works. But Rachmaninov's pay-off for compactness means that these themes, though developed, are not extended ones. The contrast with the wondrously long theme from the *Second Symphony's* third movement is certainly put into relief. There may be good reasons why the *Fourth Piano Concerto* has been overlooked. With the *Third Symphony*, however, its relative neglect is less justified, and with its economy of design, this deceptively original work is one of Rachmaninov's finest.

Rachmaninov's style modified and matured over the years, and the later works are, in reality, less melodically opulent than his earlier ones. From the mid 1920s onwards, a sense of compression prevails. The *Fourth Piano Concerto* and *Third Symphony* are cases in point, as is Rachmaninov's final composition, the *Symphonic Dances*. This started life as a two-piano version with a working title of *Fantastic Dances*. Though appropriate, its final title, and the subtitles of the three movements – *Noon, Twilight, Midnight* – do not necessarily enhance understanding the work. On the one hand, its rhythmic drive, indeed harking back to the *First Symphony*, and the waltz-like second movement, suggest some elements of cavorting, whilst on the other hand, the logic of its musical polemic belongs to the symphony.

This work shows no signs of a composer's flagging creative powers. On the contrary, there are audacious new directions here, not least in imaginative orchestration. Though some earlier works, notably the *First* and *Second* symphonies, could be said to be at times over-scored, Rachmaninov's orchestration became lighter and more transparent in the works from the *Fourth Piano Concerto* onwards. In the *Symphonic Dances,* there is a striking passage with the announcement of the central theme in the first movement. It is a saxophone solo, supported by piano which is here treated not as a soloist, but as a rank and file member of the orchestra, and ushered in by some wonderfully translucent woodwind writing which really is a product of twentieth, rather than nineteenth, century orchestral technique.

Rachmaninov's influence was not significant, but his legacy is. After all, he is amongst the most frequently performed of twentieth century composers, hence the space devoted to him here. In addition to his well-loved compositions, there are many recordings which testify to his extraordinary pianism. He was also a fine conductor, a facet of his talent which today is largely ignored, but which was, for Rachmaninov, as significant as his career as composer and pianist. He was, in effect, the last of the great composer-virtuosi.

CHAPTER 7

—

The Twentieth Century (Part II)

The Second Viennese School – Schoenberg, Berg and Webern

The music discussed so far falls under the generic description of tonal music, that is, music whose harmonic language relies on tonality. In simple terms, this means that the music is written in a key. It should be understood, however, that within these possibilities, there is an abundance of diversity and, not surprisingly, Bach's Baroque vision of tonality is far removed from Debussy's almost two hundred years later. We have already observed how Debussy was influenced by non-Western music, enabling him to break free from post-Wagnerian Austro-German syntax. Not so with Vienna born Arnold Schoenberg (1874–1951). He viewed this Austro-German tradition as dynamic and constantly evolving, and the new language that he pioneered was, for him, a natural evolution of the Wagner-Brahms tradition. As we have seen, the same was true for Richard Strauss who, although engaging in some rather daring experimentation of musical language, retreated from this, and remained true to tonality.

Schoenberg's earlier works clearly show his indebtedness to Wagner and Brahms, as well as to his contemporary Mahler. His string sextet

Verklärte Nacht (*Transfigured Night*, 1899), often performed in its version for string orchestra, is one of the few works of his known and loved by many concertgoers. For Schoenberg, though, this late Romantic tonal language was unsustainable. He was acutely aware that tonality had always been in a state of flux, always changing and redefining itself.

Previously discussed, is how Wagner, most famously in his Prelude to *Tristan and Isolde*, had sown the seeds for tonality's amorphous future, though the origins of this can be traced back to Beethoven, if not further. Wagner's reluctance to follow slavishly the rules of resolving discords onto concords, and of clearly defining keys, was Schoenberg's starting point. He took Wagner's model to its logical conclusion, and began to have whole chains of unrelated discords which never resolved, and were therefore unable to define tonality.

His language went out of its way to avoid any gestures which might imply a key, and the hierarchy of notes and chords within a key were discarded. With this, 'emancipation of the dissonance', as it has often been described, Schoenberg had discovered atonality, highly chromatic music which is not allied to any key or tonal system. By 1908, the *Five Orchestral Pieces* were the first of Schoenberg's orchestral works to use this newly evolved musical language, by way of the transitional *First Chamber Symphony* (1906), plus other chamber and vocal music.

These atonal pieces are experimental and ground-breaking. However, there was no harmonic language, with its necessary rules and traditions, for Schoenberg to hang his works onto. Tonality and structure are clearly linked. For example, sonata form relies on the tensions and relaxations of key relationships for its existence. With this type of free atonality, there are no received forms and structures and, consequently, Schoenberg was unable to sustain long musical arguments, relying, instead, on relatively short movements or sections. In effect, he had reached a compositional blind alley.

He eventually started to apply a formal system for his atonal music, where the arbitrary nature of atonalism would be governed by a strict, formalized system, now known as twelve-tone music, or serialism, as strict as the classical rules of harmony and counterpoint. His earliest reference to this system was in 1921, though he had been working on its principles for some time. In it, the music was based on the sequence of the twelve chromatic notes which the composer would arrange into what is known, variously, as a tone row, note row, or series.

This would be the basis for a particular composition, where the notes of the row would be used melodically and harmonically in succession. Additional rows would result from transposing the original row, known as the Prime, inverting the Prime and its inversions (ie, a mirror image), using it backwards (known as the retrograde), and using it backwards and inverted (retrograde-inversion), plus transposing all these different versions. Thus, a total of forty-eight rows could be derived from the Prime.

Now utilizing a system which could sustain longer atonal pieces, Schoenberg composed his finest orchestral works. These include the *Variations for Orchestra* (1928), the *Violin Concerto* (1936), and the *Piano Concerto* (1942). Added to this new musical language, was Schoenberg's use of *Klangfarbenmelodie* (tone-color melody), also employed by Mahler, where one melodic line shifts to different instruments, and where chords are defined by instrumental color as much as by pitch.

Schoenberg is something of a paradox. On the one hand, he is universally recognized as one of the foremost pioneers of modern music, whose integrity of the vision of his own beliefs confirms his place as one of the towering figures of twentieth century music. He is also remembered as an inspirational teacher, and the author of seminal volumes on music theory and composition. He felt that serialism would guarantee the supremacy of German music for generations.

On the other hand, for such an influential figure, unlike his other pioneering contemporaries such as Bartók and Stravinsky, Schoenberg's music has never won the hearts of the majority of concertgoers. For them, atonality remains something of an incoherent noise, and his orchestral works are not regular visitors to the concert platform. Interestingly, whilst never relinquishing atonality, some of his later pieces, written in the USA after he fled Nazi-occupied Europe, return to a less chromatic style, with works such as the *Theme and Variations for Full Band* (1943), which Schoenberg also arranged for orchestra, though these compositions are amongst his least exciting.

Schoenberg's innovations did not, despite his prediction, secure the supremacy of German music. For many, this new style was too restrictive and, in any case, as the twentieth century progressed, the Austro-German stranglehold over things musical waned significantly. Even so, the shape of twentieth century music would have been far different had it not been for Schoenberg, plus his two most important Vienna born students, Alban Berg (1885–1935) and, most crucially, Anton Webern (1883–1945), the three composers known collectively as the Second (or New) Viennese School, to distinguish them from the first Viennese school of Mozart, Beethoven, Schubert and others.

Berg and Webern each offered different ways forward as far as atonality and their mentor's twelve-tone technique was concerned. Their early works were tonal, followed by a period of free atonality, and culminating with their adherence to serialism. Berg is perhaps the most accessible of the Second Viennese School composers. His orchestral output is relatively meager, but within it is one of the century's masterpieces, and the only twelve-tone composition that could be described as popular – the *Violin Concerto* (1935).

The approachability of this piece is due to Berg's reliance on a tone row which has clear harmonic implications, a feature not unusual for Berg. The first three notes of the row, played simultaneously, make up a chord of G minor; notes three, four and five make up a chord of D major; a chord of A minor for notes five, six and seven; a chord of E major for notes seven to nine. The final notes make the first four notes of an ascending whole-tone scale (B, C#, D#, E#). Thus, there are familiar harmonic and melodic signposts for the listener and, indeed, Berg makes clear use of these harmonic implications. The concerto is in two movements, though with each movement being in two sections so that, in effect, there are four movements. Berg incorporates Austrian dances and folk-themes, demonstrating how he assimilates twelve-tone technique with tonal melody.

But the most striking example of this, not just in this work, but in Berg's output in general, is the second section of the second movement. Here, the three whole tones of the final notes of the tone row dovetail into the first four notes, three whole tones, of the Bach chorale *Es ist genug (It is Enough)*. There follows a set of variations based on this. These tonal signposts certainly aid the listener's enjoyment of the piece, and as the *Concerto* peacefully comes to its conclusion in a haze of lush B flat major/G minor harmonies, Schoenberg's at times astringent take on serialism seems to belong to another world.

There is also something almost programmatic about this concerto which has helped to win the hearts of audiences. The work is dedicated "To the memory of an angel", the angel being Manon Gropius, the daughter of Mahler's widow, Alma, by her second marriage to the architect Walter Gropius. Manon died from infantile paralysis at the age of nineteen just as Berg commenced work on the concerto and, as Berg was particularly close to the Gropius family, it affected him deeply. Eight months later, Berg himself died, and so it is easy to conjecture that the overt lyricism of the concerto, and its reference to the Bach chorale, quoting the words "It is enough, Lord", enshrines a type of Requiem for Berg as well as Manon. Though this is only speculation, it perhaps adds to the appeal of this sensitive work.

Berg's other purely orchestral works include the *Three Pieces for Orchestra* (1914), the *Chamber Concerto* (1925) for piano, violin and fifteen instruments, and the arrangement for strings, made in 1928, of the *Lyric Suite* (1926) originally composed for string quartet.

If Berg represents what might be described as the neo-romantic side of the Second Viennese School, Webern represents the cerebral. He is, in many ways, the most fascinating of this trio of composers. For one thing, he was the composer who most influenced the post-war modernists. Shy and retiring by nature, his music reflects his personality in its restraint and understatement. Certainly, a feature of his scores is the ubiquitous use of quiet dynamic markings. His opus numbers reach just thirty-one, and his whole output, characterized by short, indeed miniature, pieces, can be performed in around four hours. Once Webern relinquished tonality, unlike Schoenberg and Berg, he never came back to it.

He composed few pieces for full orchestra. His *Opus 1* is, for many audiences, his most accessible and popular, the post-Brahmsian *Passacaglia* (1908). In 1910, he composed his *Six Pieces for Orchestra*, and in 1913 the *Five Pieces for Orchestra*. The *Symphony* (1925), despite its title, is for chamber orchestra, as is the *Concerto for Nine Instruments*, whilst the *Orchestral Variations* (1940), were published posthumously. These last three pieces all adopt twelve-tone technique.

Webern's use of the tone row demonstrates his love for order, and for relationships to the whole, of small units within the series. In the *Symphony*, for example, notes seven to twelve are a transposed version of the retrograde of notes one to six. Or, in other words, the retrograde of the complete row is a transposed version of the Prime. In the *Concerto*, notes four to six are a retrograde inversion of notes one to three, notes seven to nine are a retrograde of one to three, and the last three are an inversion of the first three. This level of intricacy and integration is typical of Webern's later works.

Such profound control of pitch, and Webern's subtle use of *Klangfarbenmelodie*, led the immediate post-war generation, notably the Darmstadt composers, discussed later, to experiment with total serialism, whereby timbre, dynamics and rhythm would also be subjected to serial technique. Translucent textures, elaborate use of counterpoint as, for example, in the ever-present use of canon in the *Symphony*, was one outcome of his detailed study of the music of the fifteenth century Dutch composer Heinrich Isaak.

Webern's delicate artistry sets it apart from Schoenberg and Berg. Their late Austro-German Romantic heritage is evident. Webern, however, whilst considerably influenced by his teacher, went far beyond, creating an expressively transparent sound-world. Not just in his original compositions, but also in, for example, his 1935 arrangement, for chamber orchestra, of the *Ricacare* from Bach's *Musical Offering*, is this apparent.

Ives

Charles Ives (1874–1954) was one of the most astonishingly original composers of his generation. In his formative years in his native USA, there were no classical composers whose music, yet alone influence, had spread abroad. Interesting, then, that Ives should choose to look at things local, rather than international, for his inspiration. It is this very feature which marks him out to be a fascinating figure in early twentieth century music. Though he lived into the second half of the century, his significant works had largely been penned by the early 1920s. Ives composed in isolation, with many works not performed until years after their composition and, indeed, until after his death. His achievements are even more notable when we consider that he did not earn his living from music; he was an insurance broker.

His output is relatively small, and the bulk of it is chamber music and songs. Nonetheless, the orchestral works contain some of his most innovative ideas. Had he continued to compose in the style of his *First Symphony* (1898), Ives's name might well have been relegated to history's footnotes. His *Second Symphony* (1901) begins to show his experimentation in the simultaneous juxtaposition of what might be seen as opposing types of music. In this case, it is Brahms and Wagner, whose followers ensured that their rivalry would become part of musical folklore. In fact,

Ives was making the point that it is not necessarily the composers who put stylistic barriers between themselves, but their followers and, in any case, as Ives seems to be articulating, Brahms and Wagner were two sides of the same post-Beethoven coin.

But it is his use of American music, whether it be the songs of the mid-nineteenth century composer Stephen Foster, the music of marching bands, hymns, or fraternity songs, which mark him out as a nationalist composer. The *Fourth Symphony* (1916), for example, contains around two dozen popular tunes of the day. The titles of his works, too, place them thousands of miles from mainland Europe: *Central Park in the Dark* (1906); *Three Places in New England* (1914); *Washington's Birthday, Decoration Day, The Fourth of July* and *Thanksgiving* from his *Holidays Symphony* (1913). When incorporating well-known melodies, they would often be superimposed in a collage of sound. In *Central Park in the Dark*, for example, the strings offer a blanket of slow-moving chords, suggesting the velvet darkness of night, whilst snatches of melody from across the park are placed on top of that and on each other. It was a type of night music which preceded Bartók by some years.

In *The Unanswered Question* (1908), an out-of-sight muted string orchestra plays hymn-like chords, whilst a solo trumpet has its own music in a different tempo and, at the opposite side of the platform, four flutes have their own material. It should also be noted, in relation to this, that Ives's innovations really were arrived at in artistic seclusion. He was writing his own type of atonal, polytonal and polyrhythmic music not only without any knowledge of what was happening with the European *avant-garde*, but even before the innovations of Schoenberg and others. His harmonic language, for instance, includes the use of tone-clusters, rather than clearly defined chords, and quarter-tones. Long after he had more or less stopped composing in the 1920s, Ives was regarded by some as a well-meaning amateur. In his earlier years certainly, his music was too experimental for the conservative American audiences of the day. His music was neglected, and even in his later years, performances were few. An example of this is the *Fourth Symphony* which was not performed in its entirety until 1965.

Stravinsky

At the time of his death in 1971, Igor Stravinsky (1882–1971) was already considered a twentieth century master. By the turn of the new millennium, there was little doubt in the minds of many musicians that he was arguably the greatest composer of his century, something of a latter-day Beethoven. Indeed, the equivalence with Beethoven is not specious. Like the nineteenth century master, Stravinsky was not only an innovator, but someone who had a profound impact on many that came later. Had he not produced anything else after the seminal *The Rite of Spring* (often referred to by its French title of *Le Sacre du Printemps*) in 1913, his significance would still be considerable. A pupil of Rimsky-Korsakov, his early works, such as the short *Fireworks* (1908), for large orchestra, is testament to this type of Russian heritage.

It was on the basis of this work that Diaghilev invited Stravinsky to compose for his famous Ballets Russes. Diaghilev's Ballets Russes commissioned all manner of scores from contemporary composers. Debussy's *Jeux*, Ravel's *Daphnis et Chloé*, Falla's *The Three-Cornered Hat*, and Stravinsky's ballets, are just a handful. With daring choreography, innovative stage design, and a huge orchestra, these commissions enabled composers to reassess contemporary ballet. All of these scores place demands on the listener, demands that the average ballet goer was not always prepared for. In this context, the lukewarm audience response to *Daphnis et Chloé* and, a year later the notorious premiere of Stravinsky's *The Rite of Spring*, is understandable, though not forgivable.

If the rest, as they say, is history, it is one which contains an infamous premiere, when the Parisian audience rioted at the first performance of *The Rite of Spring*. Not since Beethoven's *Fifth Symphony* had rhythm been used on such a huge scale, where its emphasis was equal to that of melody, harmony and orchestral color. Of course, any Ballets Russes premiere was significant, and this one was made even more so with choreography by the most famous ballet dancer of his age, Nijinsky. The premiere has often been cited as the birth of modern dance. The visual spectacle, then, was challenging enough for the audience. But the music also made demands in ways which ballet music had not done previously. Conventional set ballet tableaux were dispensed with, and instead of woodland glades with tutued princesses, there were pagan scenes, culminating in a sacrificial virgin dancing herself to death.

The music of this score will always sound brutal and elemental. It relies on huge rhythmic patterns to sustain its thirty-five minute span, with rhythmic phrases repeated over and over again, underlined by stabs of orchestral color which replace the splashes of sound encountered in Stravinsky's first great ballet, *The Firebird* (1910). Harmonically, *The Rite of Spring* was Stravinsky's most ambitious score to date. It takes further the innovations from his previous ballet, *Petrushka* (1911), where we encounter bi-tonality – music being played in two different keys simultaneously. In *The Rite of Spring*, Stravinsky piles different harmonies on top of each other, creating a harmonic sound-world previously unheard, particularly significant as, despite the contemporaneous innovations of the Second Viennese School, *The Rite of Spring* is tonal.

Melodic lines are, for the main, relatively simple, with much emphasis placed on repetition, rather than classical-type development, and short melodic fragments – a procedure far removed from German classicism, and underlying Stravinsky's Russian musical heritage. Rhythmically, Stravinsky repeatedly changes time signatures, creating frequent natural accents at the beginning of bars. For example, during the final seventy-three bars, there are forty-five changes of meter, taking much further the metrical changes found in *Petrushka* or *The Firebird*. There is a huge orchestra, including alto flute, tenor tubas, 'piccolo' trumpet, bass trumpet, and a percussion section which calls for two timpanists. Taken individually, some aspects of Stravinsky's sound-world had been used by other composers. For instance, Richard Strauss had experimented with bi-tonality in his operas *Salome* and *Elektra* five or so years earlier. Debussy's experimentations with harmony around ten years before were every bit as daring as Stravinsky's. Schoenberg had, by 1913, managed to expunge any semblance of tonality in his music. But with *The Rite of Spring*, it seemed to be the apotheosis of all of this. Some one hundred years on since the riotous premiere of this work, *The Rite of Spring* still has something of the shock-value to it.

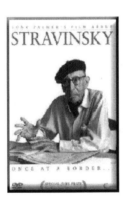

As Stravinsky approached the 1920s, he relinquished the huge, post-Russian school style, and embraced neo-classicism, an ideal spearheaded by Satie. To describe this style as 'back to Bach', as it is sometimes labelled, is to misunderstand its importance. It is true that, for example, in works such as the *Violin Concerto* (1931) and the *Dumbarton Oaks Concerto* (1938), there is more than a hint of Bach-like counterpoint and clarity of texture. However, Stravinsky, along with composers like Hindemith and Poulenc, wanted to see how the compositional techniques of the eighteenth century in particular could inform a new twentieth century musical language. The *Violin Concerto*, for example, contains movements called *Toccata*, *Aria* and *Capriccio*, and *Dumbarton Oaks* might be a concerto grosso, but there is no place for mere pastiche in these works.

On the other hand, the ballets *Pulcinella* (1920), and *The Fairy's Kiss* (1928) rely heavily on the music of Pergolesi and Tchaikovsky, respectively. Later, in the *Ebony Concerto* (1945), written for Woody Herman's big band, Stravinsky combines his own brand of neo-classical concertante style with jazz, in a work which is his most ambitious foray into jazz-influenced composition. In other neo-classical compositions, Stravinsky's innovations were in the area of using instrumental color to inform structure. For instance, in the *Symphonies of Wind Instruments* (1920), the structure is dictated by the use of instrumental blocks of sound, such as high, spiky material contrasted against low sustained sounds.

It was only after Schoenberg's death that Stravinsky started to compose works which adopted serial, twelve-tone techniques, and between 1952 and 1955, he immersed himself in the works of Webern. Until 1957, he composed a number of serial compositions, yet ones which still paid service to tonality. These works include the non-programmatic ballet *Agon* (1957) which, aesthetically, is still neo-classical, with its reliance on forms inspired by seventeenth century French dances. From the late 1950s, his serial works were less reliant on tonal areas, as he became more confident at expressing his ideas exclusively through serial techniques. In amongst the significant music from this later period is the totally serial *Movements* (1959) for piano and orchestra. One of Stravinsky's most challenging orchestral works, there is yet that unmistakable Stravinsky sound and gesture, created through timbre, color, rhythm and instrumental voicing, traceable from his first Russian ballets of some fifty years earlier.

Bartók

The Budapest premiere of Richard Strauss's *Also sprach Zarathustra* in 1902 marked a watershed in the development of Béla Bartók (1881–1945) as a composer. Until then, he had composed a number of slight and minor works. But on hearing Strauss's tone poem, he was influenced enough to embark on a number of ambitious works, including the nationalistic symphonic poem *Kossuth* in 1903. Works such as the *Piano Rhapsody* (1904) for piano and orchestra, and the *First Orchestral Suite* (1905) followed. At the same time, in 1904, he began to discover authentic Hungarian folksong. Within this short period, then, the compositional seeds were sown for someone who, though initially influenced by Liszt, Brahms, Strauss and Debussy, would become one of the most significant composers of the twentieth century.

Before Bartók, composers such as Liszt and Brahms had employed what they thought to be traditional Hungarian music. In truth, these melodies were nothing more than folk-like popular tunes. Bartók's discovery in 1904 was of a Hungarian peasant song, which he notated, sung by a young girl in rural Hungary. He soon realized that there was a rich store of indigenous music which he could use as the basis for his own compositions. The following year, he teamed up with Kodály, and together they traveled Hungary and its surrounding lands in search of folksongs, at first notating it on location, though by 1906 recording it on an Edison phonograph. This folksong revival was not peculiar to Hungary, of course. At the same time in England, Vaughan Williams and Holst were doing something similar.

What Bartók discovered in the folk music was to directly inform his compositions from then on. It led him to derive a tonal system based on modality. For example, he discovered that much Hungarian folk music was in a Lydian, or Lydian-derived, mode, characterized by its sharpened fourth degree of the scale. Thus, using white notes on the piano keyboard, this would be a scale of F to F. Of special interest, is the relationship between the tonic note (in this case F), and the fourth (B), defining the interval of the tritone. So, although music utilizing this mode is most definitely tonal, the strong characteristic of the tritone makes it decidedly un-classical. As Debussy had already discovered, and as previously noted, once non-classical tonality is used, such as scales which do not conform to the major/minor system, then standard, functional harmony, and long-term tonal structuring, cannot be employed.

Bartók also began to employ rhythmic motives derived from speech patterns peculiar to the Magyar language. Eventually, this resulted in irregular phrase lengths, and strong accents on weak beats within a regular meter, thereby, in effect, destroying a sense of meter. Interestingly, Stravinsky achieved something similar, though in his case it was through using constantly-changing time signatures.

The percussive aspect of Bartók's instrumentation was also influenced by folk music, and in particular by the indigenous instruments found therein, or by the idiosyncratic use of conventional instruments. Bartók's innovative treatment of the piano as a percussion instrument, or his invention of 'snap' pizzicato (sometimes referred to as the

'Bartók pizz'), are cases in point. In the *First Piano Concerto*, for example, he uses cluster chords, though the American composer Henry Cowell's use of these pre-dates Bartók.

Bartók was one of those artists who was particularly close to nature. Mysterious 'night music', as it is sometimes called, influenced by the sound of night creatures, and the veil of darkness, can be experienced in many of the orchestral works, including all three piano concertos (1926, 1931, 1945), *Music for Strings, Percussion and Celeste* (1936), and the *Concerto for Orchestra* (1943, revised 1945).

His most experimental music belongs to the 1920s and 1930s. In orchestral terms, this refers to the ballet, or pantomime, as Bartók described it, *The Miraculous Mandarin* (in its final version completed in 1931), the *Music for Strings, Percussion and Celeste*, and the first two piano concertos. From the *Second Violin Concerto* (1938) onwards, his style generally mellowed, capturing a newly found lyricism and warmth. The openings of the *Second Violin Concerto* and *Third Piano Concerto* are cases in point, whilst the *Concerto for Orchestra* has become a popular orchestral showpiece.

Along with Debussy, Schoenberg and Stravinsky, Bartók was undoubtedly one of the great musical movers and shakers in the first half of the twentieth century. In his use of texture, rhythm, his innovative use of instruments, most notably his string, piano and percussion writing, his highly chromatic tonal language, his mathematically proportioned structures, his utilization of folksong and the sounds of nature, he influenced various composers in many ways.

Such is Bartók's towering legacy, that the contributions of other contemporary Hungarians tend to pale. Whilst Bartók's friend Zoltán Kodály (1882–1967) is largely remembered as a seminal music educator, at least one of his orchestral works, the colorful and folkloristic *Háry János Suite* (1927) enjoys popularity, as do his *Dances from Galánta* (1933) and the *Peacock Variations* (1939). Of the orchestral works of another of Bartók's friends, Ernõ Dohnányi (1877–1960), only his *Variations on a Nursery Tune* (1914) for piano and orchestra is today regularly performed.

Other Northern Europeans and Americans

So far, the discussion of composers who were to shape the language of the twentieth century has concentrated on a small number of key figures whose influence has been considerable. These include Debussy, Schoenberg, Berg, Webern, Stravinsky and Bartók. The maverick genius Charles Ives has also been discussed, plus composers such as Elgar and Rachmaninov who represent the best of Romanticism's swansong. There is a whole host of other composers who were active immediately before and during the first half of the twentieth century and beyond. Some have orchestral works which are only occasionally performed on the international stage, whilst others have limited reputations and influence.

An example is Frederick Delius (1862–1934). Born in England, though of German extraction, he made France his home before he was 30, after briefly tending the family's plantation in Florida. He composed a large number of orchestral works, though today only a relatively small amount of the shorter pieces are regularly played. His late Romantic harmonic language is highly chromatic and rhapsodic, and unlike his English contemporary Elgar, he eschewed rigid, formal structures. A case in point would be to compare Delius's *Cello Concerto* (1921) with the almost contemporaneous Elgar *Cello Concerto*. Delius's rhapsodic style, relying on the Wagnerian concept of continuous melody, is in contrast to Elgar's tightly controlled form. This is not to suggest any lack of unity. On the contrary, Delius would employ sonata form principles, for example, for his own ends. But his use of form suited the descriptive titles of many of his orchestral works and, indeed, the titles lent themselves to freedom of form.

In his own lifetime, Delius's music was frequently performed, largely due to the championing of the British conductor Thomas Beecham. Today, the short and beautifully crafted orchestral character pieces are regularly performed at the expense of the larger works. These short works include the ecstatic *The Walk to the Paradise Garden* from the opera *A Village Romeo and Juliet* (1901), *Summer Night on the River* (1911), and *On Hearing the First Cuckoo in Spring* (1912). His amanuensis, Eric Fenby (1906–1997), must take much of the credit for saving Delius's music from obscurity. Delius's final works, including the poignant *A Song of Summer* (1930) were composed when he was blind and paralysed from syphilis, but were dictated to Fenby. Indeed, this was one of the most remarkable of musical partnerships.

Delius's friend, Australian-born Percy Grainger (1882–1961), was a folksong collector, pianist and composer. Like its creator, his music is rather eccentric, and in this he shares some similarities to Satie. Well known compositions of his are *Country Gardens*, *Molly on the Shore*, and *Handel in the Strand*. He invented what he termed 'elastic scoring', so that works could be performed using a variety of instrumental combinations, depending on what was on hand at any one time. Consequently, a large amount of his music is available in varied arrangements, though much of it started out as piano music. His orchestration, however, can be brilliantly original and idiosyncratic, frequently ignoring the 'rules', and emphasizing wayward groupings of orchestral sections, and combinations of instruments. There is often much emphasis placed on percussion. The result is wonderfully inventive and refreshing, as in the suite *In a Nutshell* (1916), his 1950 orchestration, for Leopold Stokowksi, of *Country Gardens*, or the ballet *The Warriors* (1916).

The only regularly performed orchestral work by the Swiss-American composer Ernest Bloch (1880–1959) is *Schelomo* (1916) for cello and orchestra, and subtitled *Hebrew Rhapsody*. Like Bernstein a generation later, Bloch's music is directly informed by his Jewishness. Though he did not wish to recreate whatever might be described as authentic Jewish music, the titles of many pieces, such as the *Israel Symphony* (1916), plus many chamber works, point to his deep love of his Jewish heritage.

Schelomo is rightly regarded by many as one of the century's finest compositions for cello and orchestra. Whilst the work is not strictly programmatic, it is inspired by the figure of King Solomon (the Hebrew transliteration of his name is normally Shlomo). Here, Bloch conjures up an ancient Biblical landscape which acts as a backdrop to this mighty ruler who was also a poet, lover, and philosopher. Like much of Bloch's work, the musical language is dark and ardent, with influences ranging from Richard Strauss to Debussy.

This somewhat murky language is particularly evident in, for example, the surprisingly neglected *Symphony for Trombone and Orchestra* (1954), whereas the *Voice in the Wilderness* (1936), and the orchestrated version of *Baal Shem* (1923) for violin and orchestra, are suitably exotic in their Jewishness. *Baal Shem* takes as its starting point the figure of the eighteenth century founder of the Chassidic movement. From the 1920s, Bloch embraced neo-classicism in such works as the two *Concerti Grossi* (1925 and 1952). He was also an eminent teacher, one of his most well-known students being the American composer Roger Sessions.

The music of Karol Szymanowski (1882–1937) is widely regarded in his native Poland, though some of his orchestral works, such as the two *Violin Concertos* (1916 and 1933), are not entirely absent from the world concert platform. Like Bloch, he was initially influenced by the late German Romanticism of Richard Strauss, and later adopted an impressionist style influenced by Debussy. In truth, he was something of an eclectic, being also inclined towards the more progressive harmonic language of Scriabin, as well as Polish folk music and, later, in parallel with Bloch, neo-classicism.

The French-American composer Edgard Varèse (1883–1965) should, by rights, have a chapter to himself, for he was one of the great experimenters of the twentieth century. However, many of his works belong more to the realm of chamber and ensemble music, rather than the orchestral, and his music is not widely known amongst those who frequent subscription concerts. He was initially influenced by Debussy, Schoenberg and Stravinsky, but soon started to strike out in a rather individualistic way. More than any other composer of the 1920s and 1930s, Varèse positioned his works within the context of the machine age, so that he placed a huge emphasis on percussion, underlined by uncompromising dissonance, rhythmic complexity, the negation of melodic line, and the eschewing of traditional forms and structure. This attempt to liberate language from any adherence to convention, was further assisted in the 1950s by the use of electronic tape.

Varèse's genius, then, is partly due to his attempt to blur the boundaries between music and noise. For example, in *Ionisation* (1931), noise for noise's sake is achieved by using, almost exclusively, just percussion instruments, the only other sounds being produced by two sirens – not instruments in themselves but, rather, noise-makers. In *Déserts* (1954), the recorded sound of industrial noise is incorporated around the wind and percussion. A relatively early work to use electronics, this piece marks a watershed in the post-war *avant-garde*. The premiere itself was historically significant, as two of the most important young composers of that time took part: Pierre Boulez and Karlheinz Stockhausen.

Varèse was not a prolific composer. He composed little in his later years, and the late 1930s and 1940s produced nothing. His two major orchestral works are *Amériques* (1922) and *Arcana* (1927). Interestingly, this latter piece is far more conventionally organized than others. As an orchestral sound-experience, it is remarkable, yet demanding for many an average concertgoer, though it makes only rare appearances in symphony concerts.

The most frequently performed work by the Swiss composer Frank Martin (1890–1974) is the *Petite Symphonie Concertante* (1945) for piano, harpsichord, harp and double string orchestra. Martin's style went through various changes, first being influenced by the late nineteenth century French school and impressionism, to strict serialism, via a folk-inspired period, and finally a neo-classical style combining some elements of tonality with serialism. Other notable orchestral works include the *Concerto for Wind, Timpani and Strings* (1949), the *Violin Concerto* (1951), and *Harpsichord Concerto* (1952).

The only orchestral music by German-born Kurt Weill (1900–1950) which is well known, is the orchestral suite from the opera *The Threepenny Opera* (1929), which contains one of the best-known songs ever: *Mack the Knife*. His rarely performed orchestral output includes two symphonies (1921 and 1933), and a *Violin Concerto* (1924). But he is chiefly remembered for the collaborative operas with Bertolt Brecht and, after he settled in the USA from 1935, fleeing Germany in 1933, his lighter theater works, which include the much-loved *September Song*. Ernst Krenek (1900–1991), too, fled his native Austria to settle in the USA. Like Weill, he is mainly remembered for stage music, notably the jazzy 1927 opera *Jonny spielt auf* (*Jonny Strikes up the Band*). Even so, a perusal of his works reads like a dictionary of twentieth century style, embracing as it does all the main 'isms' of the period. His list of compositions contains five infrequently performed symphonies.

Southern Europeans and Latin Americans

In the nineteenth century, there are some isolated examples of Italian orchestral music. Paganini and Rossini have already been mentioned, and to this can be added the operatic overtures of Verdi. It was not until the early twentieth century that opera's domination on Italian composers began to be replaced by orchestral works, though in terms of quantity and popularity, these cannot be compared to what was being concurrently produced in Germany or France. Indeed, even today, it seems that only the orchestral music of Ottorino Respighi (1879–1936) enjoys any lasting international popularity, and with this composer we encounter music of unarguable quality and craftsmanship. His three best known orchestral works are the impressionistic symphonic poems *The Fountains of Rome* (1917), *The Pines of Rome* (1924), and *Roman Festivals* (1929). His orchestration is sumptuous and masterly, and his sense of melody attractive and accessible. This is evident in, for example, the well-known final section of *The Pines of Rome*, an extended and expertly controlled orchestral crescendo, offering a rousing peroration.

Other Italians whose orchestral music occasionally finds a place on the international concert platform include Alfredo Casella (1883–1947) and Ildebrando Pizzeti (1880–1968). Later Italians comprise Pizzeti's pupil Mario Castelnuovo-Tedesco (1895–1968), and Goffredo Petrassi (1904–2003), whose works include eight concertos for orchestra. The importance of Gian Carlo Menotti (b.1911) rests largely on his many and significant operas. Similarly, Gian Franscesco Malipiero (1882–1973) is chiefly remembered for his vocal music, and also for his important performing editions of Monteverdi.

Of particular significance in twentieth century Italian music, is Luigi Dallapiccola (1904–1975). He was the first composer outside the Austro-German tradition to embrace serialism, though one which combines atonality with an overt, Italianate vocal lyricism. His most frequently performed works come from the main body of his output, namely vocal music. His orchestral works are relatively few. Even so, his *Partita for Orchestra* (1933), and *Variations for Orchestra* (1954) deserve to be more widely known. Dallapiccola, more so than any other Italian of his generation, had a marked influence on the next generation of important Italians, including Luciano Berio (discussed later), Aldo Clementi (b.1925), and Niccolò Castiglioni (b.1932).

In Spain, Isaac Albéniz (1860–1909), and Enrique Granados (1867–1916), are today primarily remembered for their colorful and sensitive piano music, rather than orchestral works. Some of the orchestral music of Manuel de Falla (1876–1946), however, has afforded him international fame, initially assisted by his ballet *El Amor Brujo* (*Love, The Magician*, 1915), a work which includes the famous *Ritual Fire Dance*. Here, a typical Spanish style of folk-like melodies is discernible, also evident in *Nights in the Gardens of Spain* (1915) for piano and orchestra, and the ballet *The Three-Cornered Hat* (1919), written for Diaghilev's Ballets Russes. Though Falla took advice from Debussy, and came under the spell of impressionism, there is little in his music which one associates with the more amorphous characteristics of impressionism. Instead, with its bold melodic ideas, and Ravel-inspired orchestration, there is a directness and accessible appeal. In his later works, however, such as the *Harpsichord Concerto* (1926), a sparer, neo-classical langauge is discernable.

The famous slow movement from the *Concierto de Aranjuez* (1939) for guitar and orchestra by Joaquín Rodrigo (1901–1999) is arguably the most recognizable music ever by a Spanish composer. Not just this movement, but the whole work is full of lyricism, and traditional Spanish rhythms. With its poetic poignancy, and interplay between cor anglais and guitar, it is the slow movement which lingers in the memory. Sadly, this ubiquitous piece has been used and abused in all manner of ways. Yet interestingly, although Rodrigo composed many other concertos for various instruments, it is the *Aranjuez* which has secured him a place in the hearts of music-lovers world-wide. By contrast, Rodrigo's contemporary, Roberto Gerhard (1896–1970), embraced the *avant-garde* by juxtaposing his own complex system of serialism with elements of Catalan culture. His densely-textured orchestral works include four symphonies (1953–1967).

The orchestral works of some Latin Americans make occasional appearances on the international concert scene. Particularly popular are the eight *Bachianas brasileiras* (1932–1944) by the Brazilian Heitor Villa-Lobos (1887–1959) for various instrumental and orchestral combinations. These exhibit a particularly inventive brand of neo-classicism, where Bach-like style is juxtaposed with Brazilian popular music. The instrumentation, too, is innovative. The first one, for example, is scored for eight cellos, and the well-known fifth one adds a voice to this scoring. In his earlier years, Villa-Lobos collected a great deal of traditional Brazilian folk music, and this influence permeates his music. Like the *Bachianas brasileiras*, the fourteen pieces which make up *Chôros* (1920–1929) also exploit various chamber and orchestral combinations, and again employ Brazilian popular idioms. Villa-Lobos was a prolific composer, and his orchestral music contains twelve symphonies and five piano concertos.

Another Brazilian composer and conductor, known for his exuberant folk-inspired music, is Carlos Chávez (1899–1978), whose output includes six symphonies, the second of which, *Sinfonía India* (1936) uses traditional Yaqui percussion instruments from northern Brazil. Orchestral works by the Argentinian Alberto Ginastera (1918–1983) make rare appearances, but they embrace concertos for harp (1956), piano (1961 and 1972) and violin (1963).

Vaughan Williams and the British School after Elgar

Elgar had laid down the gauntlet for other British composers to rise to the challenge of producing large scale orchestral pieces which would be internationally performed. Some, like Michael Tippett, William Walton and Benjamin Britten, to be discussed below, became respected international figures. Others, such as Richard Rodney Bennett (b.1936), who is well-known on both sides of the Atlantic, have been eclectic enough to write serious concert music as well as popular film scores. This is true, for example, of Malcolm Arnold (1921–2006), the composer of nine substantial symphonies (1949–1986), plus a number of shorter, well-known and relatively light, though dazzlingly orchestrated, pieces which, despite their somewhat conservative and accessible language, enjoy frequent performances both at home and abroad. Works such as his comedy overture *Beckus the Dandipratt* (1943), the *Tam O'Shanter Overture* (1955), the two sets of *English Dances* (1950 and 1951) and the *Guitar Concerto* (1959) are especially well-liked.

Immediately and briefly after the Great War, the music of Arthur Bliss (1903–1975) promised the shock of the new in its embrace of all that was novel and exciting from continental Europe. Interestingly, he retreated from that modernist world, and produced, instead, post-Elgarian compositions, such as *The Colour Symphony* (1922), *Music for Strings* (1935) and the ballet *Checkmate* (1937). Today, audiences remember him largely for just one work, the incidental music, especially the well-known *March*, for Alexander Korda's film *Things to Come* (1935). In 1941, Bliss became Head of Music at the BBC, and initiated the program 'Composer of the Week', which is still on air.

So, though some composers have been more successful than others in a country which continues to produce a wealth of new music, like some good wines, much of it has traveled badly. It would, then, be difficult to find performances of music by, for instance, Arnold Bax (1883–1953) beyond the UK, despite his wonderfully evocative and rich tone poem *Tintagel* (1917). Indeed, even his seven symphonies are infrequently performed at home.

The same is true of a whole host of British composers who, although enjoying a limited reputation in the UK, are hardly known outside it. They are too numerous to cite them all, but they include symphonists such as Havergal Brian (1876–1973) who composed thirty-six symphonies, Irish born Hamilton Harty (1879–1941), whose *Irish Symphony* (1904, revised 1915 and 1924) once enjoyed some reputation, Edmund Rubbra (1901–1986), Lennox Berkeley (1903–1989), William Alwyn (1905–1985), George Lloyd (1913–1998), Robert Simpson (1921–1997) and John McCabe (b.1939), and others such as Frank Bridge (1879–1941), who taught Benjamin Britten, John Ireland (1879–1962) and Alan Rawsthorne (1905–1971). One composer who had a brief reign of immense popularity, largely due to his choral work *The Rio Grande* (1929), was Constant Lambert (1905–1951). Though this work is still performed by British choral societies, Lambert is now chiefly remembered for his witty and readable book on contemporary music, *Music Ho!* (1931).

There are also those British composers whose reputation largely rests on one or two works, yet whose music enjoys popularity and respect. George Butterworth (1885–1916), killed in action on the Somme, is well-known for his settings of A.E. Housman. He completed only four beautifully crafted, lyrical and folksy orchestral works, between 1910 and 1911: the rhapsody *A Shropshire Lad* which, as the title might suggest, quotes from his Housman settings; *Two English Idylls*; *The Banks of Green Willow*. Philip Heseltine (1894–1930), who wrote under the name of Peter Warlock, similarly composed much vocal music, for which he is mainly known. Popular, though, is his *Capriol Suite* (1926) for strings, which draws on Arbeau's sixteenth century dance manual, *Orchésographie*, for its material.

For many music lovers, the name Gustav Holst (1874–1934) is well enough known, though probably on account of just one work, the symphonic suite *The Planets* (1916). The first movement, *Mars, the Bringer of War*, has been overused by film and documentary makers, and its style copied for many a cinematographic scene, though this should not undermine the work's value. *The Planets* is replete with brutal excitement, as in *Mars*, ethereal orchestration, as in *Saturn, the Bringer of Old Age* or *Neptune, the Mystic*, quixotic orchestration, as in *Mercury, the Winged Messenger* or *Uranus, the Magician*, and rousing melodies such as in *Jupiter, the Bringer of Jollity*, which incorporates Holst's well-known hymn tune *I Vow to Thee My Country*.

The popularity of *The Planets* is not merely due to the programmatic nature, where each of the seven movements attempts to capture the astrological description of the then known planets. The music is bold, and this from a composer who at the time was an unknown, parochial music teacher and conductor of local choirs. Even the first performance of *The Planets* was a private affair, organized by friends. One would assume, from looking at, and listening to, the score, that this was the work of a composer with some experience at writing for large orchestras, whereas the opposite is true. Influences in *The Planets* are self-evident, and these include, most obviously, Debussy and Stravinsky. In this sense, Holst's devices are derivative, and whilst this work may be something of a flawed masterpiece, it has achieved huge popularity.

Holst's other influences were folk song, which he discovered with Vaughan Williams, and Sanskrit literature. He also had some knowledge of Indian music theory. His later works exhibit a bleakness which was not always apparent earlier on, and these include the Thomas Hardy-inspired tone poem *Egdon Heath* (1927), where the opulence of *The Planets* seems to be a lifetime away. Holst's output was small, with much of it not frequently played. However, some pieces are concert favorites, including the suite from the opera *The Perfect Fool* (1922), and two pieces for strings – the *St. Paul's Suite* (1913) and the *Brook Green Suite* (1933).

The nine symphonies of Ralph Vaughan Williams (1874–1958) rank amongst the finest of the century. This is not to say, though, that his first three symphonies, *A Sea Symphony* (1910), *A London Symphony* (1920, revised 1953), and *A Pastoral Symphony* (1922, revised 1953) are as significant as contemporary symphonies by Sibelius. Nonetheless, with his great middle trilogy symphonies – the *Fourth in F minor* (1935), the *Fifth in D* (1943), the *Sixth in E minor* (1948) – we have symphonies which are at least as equal and significant as those being produced at the same time by Prokofiev, Shostakovich or Hindemith.

Like Bartók and Kodály, Vaughan Williams and his friend Gustav Holst, began collecting folksongs in the early years of the twentieth century. For Vaughan Williams in particular, this type of music was to directly inform his style. He so assimilated it, that what seem like authentic folk melodies, are often entirely new tunes. The middle section of *A Pastoral Symphony's* third movement is a case in point, where its mixolydian mode suggests it has strayed from a Home Counties village green, whereas it is an entirely original melody. Another influence was English church music, and the music from Tudor England. Between 1904 and 1906, Vaughan Williams prepared an anthology of Anglican hymns, which became famously known as *The English Hymnal*. He himself said that whilst working on it, he came across some of the best – and worst – tunes in the world.

By the time of the *Fourth Symphony*, melodic and harmonic devices originating from folk music, plus the modality found in church music, had been entirely integrated into one of the most tautly argued symphonies of the period. There is little sign here of the pastoral or pictorial which pervaded the earlier works. Instead, there is dissonance, brutality and aggression, with musical motives derived from a transposed version of BACH (ie, B flat, A, C, B natural), and quartal melodic lines, using the interval of the fourth, and thereby placing it firmly within the context of twentieth century tonal compositional technique.

If the *Fourth* is Vaughan Williams's most modernist symphony, then the *Fifth* is his most spiritual. His knowledge of Anglican church music was, as outlined above, intimate. Yet although he was the son of a clergyman, and composed a large amount of church and religious music, Vaughan Williams had little time for organized religion. However, the *Fifth Symphony* draws upon music for the as yet incomplete opera *The Pilgrim's Progress* (1951). This idea of incorporating music from an opera dealing with Bunyan's allegory of a spiritual quest, was arguably not coincidental. Moreover, the climax of the first movement clearly makes reference to the church melody *Sine Nomine*, whilst the imitative counterpoint of the last movement recalls the music of a great cathedral choir. It should be understood that the work was composed, premiered and broadcast during World War II, at a time when many would have been trying to cling on to their own individual spiritual quests during the darkest hours of the twentieth century. The peaceful, noble and life-affirming music of the *Fifth Symphony* would undoubtedly have assisted many in their search.

There is, too, a certain classicism in this work. It is dedicated "without permission" to Sibelius. Compare the quiet horn calls which open Sibelius's own *Fifth Symphony*, with Vaughan Williams's opening horn calls, both ideas having their origins in the openings of classical Romantic works such as Brahms's *Second Symphony*, or the symphonies of Bruckner. With its modestly sized orchestra, classical structures, a passacaglia finale recalling the similar device used in the finale of Brahms's *Fourth Symphony*, this is Vaughan Williams's most 'classical' symphony. There is good reason, then, why a dedication to Sibelius was appropriate, one twentieth century symphonic master paying tribute to another.

Vaughan Williams himself cautioned against ascribing programs to his middle symphonies. But hindsight is a wonderful thing, and it is therefore difficult not to consider the pre-war *Fourth Symphony* as a harbinger of terror, and the *Fifth* as a beacon of hope during that terror. The *Sixth Symphony*, inevitably, has been thought of as a vision of post-war destruction. It is hard, when listening to the constant, eerie *pianissimo* of the poignantly numbing *Epilogue*, not to conjure up war-ravaged waste-lands, and the emotional impotence felt in a post-Auschwitz world.

If for nothing else, the *Fourth*, *Fifth* and *Sixth* symphonies demonstrate that Vaughan Williams was a twentieth century master. Other orchestral works of his are particularly popular, such as the *Fantasia on Greensleeves* from the opera *Sir John in Love* (1929), *The Lark Ascending* (1914) for violin and orchestra, and the *English Folk Song Suite* (1923), in its orchestral version by Gordon Jacob. Two other orchestral works from his large output are equally as fine as the middle symphonies. They are the much loved *Fantasia on a Theme by Thomas Tallis* (1910, revised 1923) for double string orchestra and string quartet, and the ballet *Job: A Masque for Dancing* (1930).

On the one hand, *Job* inhabits that visionary and spiritual world that is later found in the *Fifth Symphony*, and on the other hand, the tautness of its musical language begins to look ahead to the *Fourth Symphony*. In its portrayal of a humble man at odds with God, and God's majesty contrasted with the corruption of Satan's music, nowhere else in Vaughan Williams's music do we find such concentrated drama, immensity and power. The *Fantasia on a Theme by Thomas Tallis* is one of a number of great twentieth century works for string orchestra by British composers. The original phrygian mode melody by the important Tudor composer Thomas Tallis was discovered by Vaughan Williams when he was working on *The English Hymnal*. The *Fantasia* has a particularly architectural sweep, and with its huge arches of sound and sonorous string writing, it is almost a musical depiction of the interior of a great medieval English cathedral. Indeed, it was premiered in such a place – Gloucester Cathedral.

Vaughan Williams's influence was to usher in what is sometimes referred to as the English pastoral school. Though many have tried to emulate his style, this school, whilst producing some worthy music, has, unfortunately, also produced that which is pleasant at best, though aimless and vapid at worst. Yet, Vaughan Williams was also a supportive teacher, his pupils including the composers Gordon Jacob (1895–1984), and the New Zealand composer Douglas Lilburn (1915–2001), whose own *Second Symphony* (1951, revised 1974), despite infrequent performances, is something of a minor masterpiece.

Walton, Tippett and Britten

The music of three British composers active immediately before, and well after, World War II, has now established itself as regular orchestral fare. They are William Walton (1902–1983), Michael Tippett (1905–1998), and Benjamin Britten (1913–1976). None of them were great innovators, though Britten's flair for experiment is largely in the realm of his many operas which form the backbone of his output. All three were tonal composers, with Britten's tonality informed by the highly chromatic type found in Berg and, particularly in his later works, a spareness of melodic line and counterpoint found in his friend Shostakovich's later works. Tippett's use of tonality, too, tends to be highly chromatic, especially in his middle period works. In terms of melodic shape, often relying on chains of the interval of the fourth, it recalls Hindemith. There are also references to Stravinsky, jazz and English Tudor polyphony. Walton's language is the most conventional of the three, a type of post-Elgarian, at times nostalgic, post-Romantic language. Even so, in the finale of his *Second Symphony* (1960), he proves a point by composing a passacaglia which skilfully uses a tone row in a particularly tonal way.

Walton's orchestral output is relatively meager as, indeed, is his general list of works. It is perhaps difficult to understand now why he was considered to be something of the *enfant terrible* of British music in the 1920s and 1930s. Works such as the entertainment for voice and small ensemble, *Façade* (1922), or the oratorio *Belshazzar's Feast* (1931), were seen as extremely modernist. And perhaps they were, when compared to the relatively tame music of the English pastoralists of the time, Vaughan Williams excepted.

In its incarnation as an orchestral suite, *Façade* is a familiar item in orchestral concerts. In this adaptation, without narrator, Walton's music does not have to play second fiddle to Edith Sitwell's inventive nonsense verse of the original version. Consequently, without the distraction of the narrator, Walton's influences are clearer to hear in the orchestral arrangement. These are wide: Stravinsky, certainly in terms of rhythm, plus jazz, some Satie-like humor, and some *Pierrot Lunaire*-type surrealism from Schoenberg. Even without knowing its name or composer, the *Popular Song* from *Façade* will be familiar to many.

Similarly memorable, and written in the same vein as Elgar's *Pomp and Circumstance* marches, is the Coronation March *Crown Imperial* (1937), composed for the coronation of King George VI. Walton's music became further familiar to the wider public when he composed film scores for Olivier's famous Shakespeare films: *Henry V* (1944); *Hamlet* (1947); *Richard III* (1955). Extracts from this music often find their way onto the concert platform, especially *Touch Her Soft Lips*, and *The Death of Falstaff* from *Henry V*.

Walton's *First Symphony in B flat minor* (1935) can stand alongside its exact contemporary, Vaughan Williams's *Fourth Symphony*, as one of the finest symphonies of the century. Its influences are plain to hear. For example, the arresting opening, with its slowly unfolding, long melodic line, recalls Sibelius, as does the closely argued huge sonata form which follows, whose structure is assisted by means of Sibelian-like pedal points. This is not to suggest any lack of originality on Walton's part. Rather, it demonstrates his engagement with post-Sibelian symphonic logic, and the way in which, for Walton, that could sustain the symphony as a genre. Similarly, the Stravinskian rhythms of the second movement, or the Hindemith-like shape of the finale's fugal section, are merely starting points to sustain this fine work.

By the time he composed his *Second Symphony*, Walton was living on his island paradise of Ischia in the Bay of Naples. This unjustly neglected work, though perhaps understandably overshadowed by the *First Symphony*, seems to capture the shimmering textures of the sultry Mediterranean which Walton could see from his now famous garden at La Mortella. This is also true of other later works, such as the *Cello Concerto* (1957). The *Violin Concerto* (1939, orchestration revised 1943 and 1950) has become something of a twentieth century concerto warhorse. Written for Heifetz, Walton himself considered it his favorite work. Again, it demonstrates his eclecticism in the way in which it pays homage, perhaps not intentionally, to violin concertos by Sibelius and Elgar in particular, and also Mendelssohn and Tchaikovsky. Within five years of each other, three of the most lyrical and poignant violin concertos were composed: in addition to Walton's, Berg's appeared in 1935, and

Samuel Barber's was to follow Walton's by a few months. All three have become much loved concert pieces.

Michael Tippett was launched to fame by his oratorio *A Child of Our Time* (1941), a work born out of his deeply held pacifist beliefs, and his disbelief in what was happening, especially to the Jews, in the name of Germany's National Socialism. In a creative life which spanned most of his century, Tippett was intensely affected by world events, and the social conditions arising from these. He often articulated his beliefs and ideas, though rarely talked about the notes themselves; of his creative processes and stylistic aesthetic, Tippett said little. Many extra-musical events influenced him. As a young man, he joined the Communist Party; during World War II, he was imprisoned as a conscientious objector; at a time when it was illegal, he did not hide his homosexuality.

If Walton was a one-time *enfant terrible* of British music, then Tippett became the angry young man. Eventually, though, he turned out to be part of the musical establishment, did a huge amount of work with young musicians, was generous with his advice for all who sought it, was bestowed with countless state honors, and ended his long life as the much-loved Grand Old Man of British Music. His influence on the younger generation of British composers is incalculable. In this respect, his position in the UK is probably similar to that of Olivier Messiaen in France, and Elliott Carter in the USA.

A case in point, to demonstrate how the contemporary world influenced his art, is the *Third Symphony* (1970). It quotes Beethoven's *Choral Symphony*, and challenges to what extent great art and culture – with Beethoven here being used as the paradigm – can have any value in a post-holocaust world. The argument here is that the holocaust was masterminded by so-called cultured people.

Tippett composed four symphonies. Whilst the *First* (1945) is now rarely performed, and whilst the *Third* is a product of its time, complete with the iconic Martin Luther King "I have a dream" quote, the *Second* (1957) is his most Classical in concept. Tippett was influenced by all manner of musical stimuli, from the Tudor music of Orlando Gibbons, to blues and jazz, via incidental music for American television films, Indonesian gamelan music, to Beethoven. Throughout his life, Tippett was somewhat fixated by Beethoven's handling of large-scale structure by means of extended sonata form, and how this could be relevant for a composer in the second half of the twentieth century. Of course, he was part of a tradition, grappling with the same problem that so intrigued the post-Beethoven symphonists, such as Brahms, Mahler and Sibelius.

In the *Second Symphony*, more so than any other orchestral work, Tippett meets the challenge head on, to produce a post-modernist, post-Romantic symphony that is cast in a Beethovenian mould. By contrast, the *Fourth Symphony* (1977) is in one continuous movement. This is a birth-to-death piece, complete with the sound of human breathing (usually produced digitally, or sampled), cyclic in form. It contains some of Tippett's most arresting music, plus remarkable orchestration, not least the vertiginous horn writing, specifically conceived for the Chicago Symphony Orchestra who commissioned the work. It remains one of the most original symphonies of the century's last quarter.

Between the late 1950s and early 1970s, Tippett composed much of his most challenging music. The later works, such as the *Triple Concerto* (1979) for violin, viola and cello, and *The Rose Lake – A Song Without Words* (1993), recapture the rapturous and luminous lyricism found in the earlier works, such as the *Fantasia Concertante on a Theme of Corelli* (1953) for strings, which is a startling example of this. Part of that rich tradition of British string pieces, its imaginative and resonant use of the string orchestra is a mature companion to the earlier and popular *Concerto for Double String Orchestra* (1939). The life-affirming and optimistic music of the opera *The Midsummer Marriage* (1952) finds its way into the orchestral repertoire by way of the four well known *Ritual Dances*.

Apart from the ever popular *The Young Persons' Guide to the Orchestra*, one mainly associates Benjamin Britten with vocal music and, in particular, opera. Indeed, he is regarded by many as the greatest operatic genius of his age. Even his non-operatic works for voice, which are outside the scope of this book, such as the *Serenade* (1943) for tenor, horn and strings, are often cited before any of the orchestral ones. Moreover, to underline this vocal aspect, his solo works for voice, and the leading male operatic characters, were written for his life-partner, the eminent tenor Peter Pears.

Along with Walton and Tippett, Britten reacted against the somewhat prevalent English pastoralism, being eager to take on board the new music from Europe, in particular Bartók and Stravinsky. He studied with the respected British composer Frank Bridge, and was to pay tribute to his teacher with his *Variations on a Theme by Frank Bridge* (1937) for strings. In fact, the majority of his orchestral works were all largely written by the end of the 1940s, with the exception of the exotically-inspired ballet *The Prince of the Pagodas* (1956) and the dark-hued *Cello Symphony* (1963).

The lighter side of Britten's orchestral style is exemplified by, for example, the early *Simple Symphony* (1934) for strings, and *Soirées*

Musicales (1936), based on music by Rossini. On the other hand, the *Violin Concerto* (1939, revised 1958) and *Sinfonia da Requiem* (1940) are deeply felt and weighty works.

Popular since its premiere as part of a documentary film, is *The Young Persons' Guide to the Orchestra* (1946), which has the wordy subtitle of *Variations and Fugue on a Theme by Purcell*. Like Prokofiev's *Peter and the Wolf*, composed some ten years earlier, it is an educational piece which introduces the instruments and sections of the orchestra. In its version for narrator and orchestra, it is wonderfully didactic, lacking any of today's *penchant* for 'dumbing down'. Without the narrator, it stands on its own as a skilful set of variations. The final section alone is an orchestral *tour de force* where, within an adroitly managed rapid fugue, Purcell's slow theme is heard as a counterpoint.

Much of Britten's music, whether for orchestra, theater or chamber, is in the regular repertoire. The most often performed orchestral music, however, are the *Four Sea Interludes* from what is one of the most frequently staged twentieth century operas, *Peter Grimes* (1945). Britain, being an island, has something of a tradition for producing music about the sea, with Britten's own teacher, Bridge, having composed an orchestral suite *The Sea* (1912).

Britten's challenge in *Dawn*, the first of the *Sea Interludes*, was to ensure that his day-break did not resemble Debussy's in *La Mer*. In the latter, the vision is dynamic, in that it plots the progress of the sun rising, and thence towards midday. It is a canvas devoid of humans. With Britten, his dawn is a snapshot in time, and a backdrop to the opera's human activity. Debussy's music rises from its low opening, *crescendos* and becomes faster. Britten's opening is more solitary, the extremely high violin line perhaps portraying a high, lone sea-bird at the start of its day. This high, rhythmically fluid line, is contrasted with low, sustained sounds, supported by brass and rumbling bass drum, suggesting the sea's depth. Clarinets, harp and violas have swirly, arabesque figures, here evoking the tide's movement. Arch-like in shape, this movement ends as it began.

This is the wonderfully controlled genius of this piece, and marks it out as something of a twentieth century masterwork. It would be easy for any composer to fall into the trap of employing well-worn musical clichés in such music. But Britten's representation of the sea is devoid of this. We have already observed that Wagner's non-vocal music within his operas is of equal worth to the vocal music. Likewise, the *Sea Interludes*, plus the *Passacaglia* from the opera, demonstrate that Britten, as Tippett did with his *Ritual Dances*, was one of the few composers to also achieve this.

Messiaen and the French School after Debussy

Erik Satie (1866–1925) was a huge influence on many French composers at the time. He outlived Debussy by some seven years, and was not only significant in his own lifetime, but was to have a profound effect on numerous composers who would sustain French music into the middle years of the century. Debussy and Ravel were immensely impressed by the music of this colorful eccentric, and they also did much to champion it. Satie's music is a suitable foil to the impressionistic complexities of Debussy. Its straightforward melodic lines, however, hide astonishing inventiveness in terms of musical notation, melodic shape, harmonic technique, and quirky titles. The only orchestral work which is performed regularly, is the ballet *Parade* (1917). It was written for the Ballets Russes, and brought together some of the most influential artists of the day: the polyglot Jean Cocteau, who gave Satie the idea to write the piece, choreographer Massine, and Picasso for the stage designs. For audiences, its most novel feature is the inclusion of a typewriter in the scoring.

With Satie's anti-Impressionist, anti-Romantic stance, he was, in truth, the first of the Neo-classical composers. Stravinsky is usually credited as being the founder of this movement, but just as we owe it to Satie for luring Debussy away from his early Wagnerian style, so we also owe it to him for encouraging Stravinsky to move away from the late Romantic style which gave rise to his Diaghilev ballets. Neo-classicism drew its influence from reacting against the overblown rhetoric of the late nineteenth century, instead turning to the clearer textures and structures of the Baroque and Classical. This is plain to hear in Satie's music.

As well as being the founder of Neo-classicism – as much as it is possible to label individuals as founders of artistic movements – he was the father figure for a group of young French composers who became known as *Les Six*, a title coined in 1920 by the critic Henri Collet. They were: Darius Milhaud (1892–1974); Arthur Honegger (1892–1955); Francis Poulenc (1899–1963); Louis Durey (1888–1979); Georges Auric (1899–1983); Germaine Tailleferre (1892–1983), who was the only female member of the group at a time when women composers were few and far between.

Poulenc, and to some extent Milhaud, became leading composers of the twentieth century. Honegger is chiefly remembered for his symphonic poem *Pacific 231* (1923), a vivid description of a train journey, and a work which extols the virtues of the machine age. The music of Durey, Auric and Tailleferre is rarely performed outside France. The two most well-known pieces of Milhaud are the ballets *Le Boeuf sur le toit* (*The Ox on the Roof*, 1920), and *La Création du monde* (*The Creation of the World*, 1923). Both demonstrate Milhaud's fascination with jazz, which he heard firsthand on a visit to Harlem in 1918, and are among several pieces of that period where jazz idioms are introduced into concert music.

Part of this neo-classical French tradition embraced other composers active in the first half of the twentieth century. These include Albert Roussel, who composed four symphonies between 1904 and 1934. In her younger years, Nadia Boulanger (1887–1979), who became the most famous and well-respected composition teacher of the century, was making a name as a composer. She stopped composing when her sister Lili (1893–1918) died, Lili herself being a composer of prodigious talent and promise.

The music of Poulenc is the most widely performed of *Les Six*. Relatively few of his orchestral works are in the regular repertoire, the vocal and chamber works being more frequently heard. Of the orchestral pieces which are performed, they demonstrate Poulenc's faithful allegiance to neo-classicism and, therefore, the ideals of *Les Six*. They are direct in approach, relying on Classical structures, clear tonality, and often employing harmonic devices derived from the Baroque. His most well-known orchestral works are the witty *Concerto for Two Pianos* (1932), which has more than a hint of Mozart in its slow movement, the ballet music *Les Biches* (1924), and the impressive and rather seriously gothic *Organ Concerto* (1938), somewhat influenced by the organ works of Bach and the Baroque composer Buxtehude. Indeed, this is one of Poulenc's finest and original works.

The *Turangalila-Symphony* (1949) by Olivier Messiaen (1908–1992) is probably the most frequently performed of any post-World War II French orchestral work. With its rapturous epic grandness and exoticism, it has understandably won the hearts of a global audience. This in itself is interesting when one considers that Messiaen, who was to influence a whole generation of younger composers world-wide, was at the forefront of musical innovation. Messiaen's influences are extensive. They include music of non-Western cultures, such as Indonesia and India, informing instrumental color and the use of irregular rhythms, respectively. Birdsong, and the composer's own deeply held Roman Catholic faith, are two other significant influences and, like Bach, Messiaen considered that his role as a musician was central to his service to God.

His musical language demonstrates elements of total serialism on the one hand, and a static type of tonality based on modes of limited transposition, on the other hand, supported by repetition of melodic fragments, and by ostinato. The modes offer a system whereby one can only transpose on to different notes a series of modes before the exact same notes are used again. Consequently, a sense of harmonic unity is clear to hear.

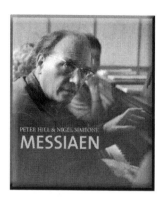

Turangalila-Symphony is a symphony in its broadest sense, in that it is a large, orchestral multi-movement work. It should not be viewed as a twentieth century symphony in the same way as those of Sibelius, Tippett or Shostakovich, which rely on classical formulas and a certain symphonic 'house-style'. *Turangalila* demonstrates that the term 'symphony' has meant many things in the twentieth century. The word *Turangalila* is Sanskrit, and defines rhythmic formulas of ancient Indian music: *Turanga* meaning 'time which runs', and *lila* meaning 'divine action' and 'love'. The rhythmic aspect of the work, in essence the *Turanga*, is most extensively demonstrated in the ecstatic and joyous fifth movement, *Joie du sang des étoiles* (*Joy of the Blood of the Stars*). To match the massive ten movement span of this eighty minute work, Messiaen uses huge forces, including two soloists: piano, and ondes martenot, the latter being an electronic keyboard instrument which is characterized by its swooping glissando sounds, and which symbolizes the 'love' music.

Chronochromie (*The Color of Time*,1960) for orchestra, demonstrates the most extensive use of Messiaen's preoccupation with birdsong in an orchestral piece. Here, birds from all over the world come together to create a bird-harmony, though one based on Messiaen's own harmonic language. It also confirms Messiaen's assertion that, for him, nature contained the true music. And for Messiaen, God was in nature. So, works such as *Couleurs de la Cité Céleste* (*Colors of the Celestial City*, 1964) for piano, wind and percussion, *Et exspecto resurrectionem mortuorum* (1964) for thirty-four wind plus percussion, or *Des canyons aux étoiles* (*From the Canyons to the Stars,* 1975) for piano and orchestra, are not explicitly nature pieces like *Chronochromie* or *Oiseaux exotiques* (*Exotic Birds*,1956) for piano, wind, and percussion. They are nonetheless expressing a connection to God through purely orchestral, non-vocal, music. In fact, Messiaen also held the post of organist at La Sainte Trinité in Paris from 1930 until his death, and much of his output was devoted to organ music.

Henri Dutilleux (b.1916) carried Roussel's mantle, becoming the foremost French symphonist of a generation which had eschewed this genre. Dutilleux discarded all his works written before the mid-1940s, after which his music displays a variety of influences, Debussy and Ravel certainly, plus Roussel. Around this time, too, he began to examine Webern's music, and consequently he veered towards an atonal style. Even so, Dutilleux's music is not easy to categorize, himself being reluctant to ally his music to any one style or school, and later works re-embraced tonality. His two symphonies (1951 and 1959) are important in that the twentieth century French symphony is not well represented on the international concert scene, and they were written at a time when leading French composers, such as Messiaen and Boulez, were striving to dispense with classical titles. Other orchestral works include the *Violin*

Concerto, L'arbre des songes (*The Tree of Dreams*,1985), *The Shadows of Time* (1997), and the *Nocturne for Violin and Orchestra, Sur un même accord* (*On the One Chord*, 2002).

Prokofiev

Apart from Sergey Prokofiev (1891–1953) and Shostakovich, there are few Soviet composers whose orchestral works have found their way into the popular concert repertoire. The spectacular music from the ballet *Spartacus* (1954, revised 1968) by the Armenian Aram Khachaturian (1903–1978) has rightly become something of a favorite, as has the well-known *Sabre Dance* from his ballet *Gayane* (1942). Music by Dmitri Kabalevsky (1904–1987) and Nicolai Miaskovsky (1881–1950) can occasionally be found on orchestral concert programs. It is Prokofiev and Shostakovich, though, who carry the weight of the finest and most frequently performed Soviet music.

Prokofiev lived for a time in France and the USA before finally resettling in the Soviet Union. Unlike Shostakovich, he came into direct contact with all that was new and exciting in terms of modern composition on both sides of the Atlantic. However, the only contemporary who significantly influenced him, was Stravinsky. Like Stravinsky, Prokofiev was a pioneer in terms of neo-classicism. His *First Symphony in D, Classical*, appeared in 1917, a year before Stravinsky's *The Soldier's Tale*, and three years before *Pulcinella*. The *Classical Symphony* was Prokofiev's response to his speculation as to what type of work Haydn might have written had he still been alive. Its Haydnesque gaiety mixed with stylistic satire, belies its sophistication, and it remains one of the most significant, and indeed fascinating, of neo-classical works. The *Classical Symphony* aside, Stravinsky's influence can be observed in Prokofiev's rhythmic drive, dissonance juxtaposed with overt diatonicism, wide-ranging melodic lines, and orchestration which is often brilliant and more daring than that of Shostakovich. This is especially apparent in the earlier orchestral works, such as the *Scythian Suite* (1915), and the *Second Symphony in D minor* (1925).

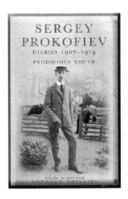

Many of Prokofiev's orchestral pieces are well established, yet some of the larger compositions have been neglected by audiences and performers alike. For example, in addition to the compositions mentioned above, the *Classical* and *Fifth Symphony in B flat* (1944), are his two most popular works in this genre. The *Fifth Symphony*, dedicated, in Prokofiev's own words, "to the spirit of man", is an appropriate companion to the best symphonies of Shostakovich. The other symphonies, however, are less frequently performed. The two violin concertos – the *First in D* (1917), and the *Second in G minor* (1935) – with their mixtures of overt lyricism, playfulness and sardonicism, are popular. The six piano concertos span a creative period of more than forty years. At the expense of the other piano concertos, the *Third in C* (1921) has established itself as a twentieth century classic, containing as it does dazzling virtuosity within an accessible, intensely melodic twentieth century language.

Indeed, this mixture of an abundance of melody, a warm, chromatically inflected harmonic language, rhythmic drive, musical humor, and skilful orchestration, characterize those works of his which have become so popular. Individual sections of works, too, have also established themselves as favorite orchestral 'lollipops', such as the *March* from the orchestral suite from the opera *The Love for Three Oranges* (1919, revised 1924), or the *Troika* from the *Lieutenant Kijé Suite* (1934). His skill at orchestration is ably exemplified in the ever popular and charming *Peter and the Wolf* (1936), which is an entertaining and educational children's guide to the orchestra.

Prokofiev composed a number of ballets, four of them for Diaghilev. The fairytale magic of *Cinderella* (1944) is an obvious example of how Prokofiev had discarded his modernist persona by the time he returned to the Soviet Union. This is in stark juxtaposition to earlier ballet scores such as *Chout* (1920) or the *Scythian Suite*. By far, his most well-known ballet score is *Romeo and Juliet* (1936). Unlike so many ballets which are no longer performed in the theater, this ballet is frequently performed on stage, and in the concert hall in the form of the two suites. The musical language is not particularly daring, and the compositional gestures which support the passion, anguish and general drama might hark back to the nineteenth century, and in particular Tchaikovsky. Yet it is well controlled, and the material, even in short, connecting numbers, is of a consistently high quality, supported by some of Prokofiev's finest orchestration. There is, then, good reason why this much loved score is regarded by many to be his finest.

Hindemith

Paul Hindemith (1895–1963) is an interesting figure, for though he is regarded as a significant leader in twentieth century music, only a small amount of orchestral music from this prolific composer is regularly performed. As well as his compositions, he is also remembered as a virtuoso viola player, and an important educationalist. His output is characterized by two important features. Firstly, along with Stravinsky, he was at the vanguard of neo-classicism. Secondly, he felt that the contemporary composer should actively engage in writing music for amateurs, or for domestic use, or for instruments which have a limited repertoire. This type of Hindemith aesthetic has become known as *Gebrauchsmusik* – 'music for use', or 'utility music'.

His style is somewhat eclectic, drawing from his own Austro-German tradition. He favored large, classical forms, and so in this respect the Beethoven-Brahms tradition is evident. But he also employed a highly chromatic type of counterpoint, informed by, though of course stylistically different from, Bach. At his most chromatic, Hindemith's music might veer towards atonality, but in fact, he never relinquished tonality. Instead, he emphasized melodic shapes and harmonies built of fourths, combining this particularly twentieth century approach with conventional triadic harmony, and in this he shares some common ground with Bartók.

Many regard his masterpiece to be the opera *Mathis der Maler* (*Mathis the Painter*, 1934), and his most well-known orchestral work is undoubtedly the symphony of the same name which he extracted from the opera's music in 1934. The *Mathis der Maler Symphony* is considered to be his finest orchestral work. The opera is about the medieval German painter Matthias Grünewald, and the symphony's three movements are titled after the panels in his Isenheim alterpiece. By way of an introduction to Hindemith, this is a particularly accessible piece. Whilst the music is drawn from the opera, and is, by necessity, programmatic, Hindemith was keen to organize his material in a symphonic way.

Likewise with the *Symphonic Metamorphosis on Themes of Carl Maria von Weber* (1943). Here, a number of themes by Weber are taken and symphonically developed to produce something of an orchestral showpiece. Despite its ponderous title, this work is perhaps Hindemith's most popular orchestral composition. Like the *Mathis Symphony*, the *Symphonic Metamorphosis* demonstrates that Hindemith's style began to mellow by the mid-1930s.

His other orchestral pieces are less frequently performed, but those that are include the *Konzertmusik* (1930) for strings and brass, the folk-song inspired *Third Viola Concerto*, *Der Schwanendreher* (1935), and the *Symphony in E flat* (1940), which is the first of five symphonies. Although he composed a number of concerto-like *Kammermusik* (literally chamber music) pieces in the 1920s, he waited until 1939 to compose the first of eight concertos for various instruments, which have their roots in the nineteenth century Romantic concerto tradition. The first of these was the *Violin Concerto*, and the last was the *Organ Concerto* (1962).

Having been attacked by Hitler's Nazi regime, Hindemith left Germany in 1937, eventually settling in the USA where he took up a professorship at Yale. Lukas Foss was amongst his pupils. In truth, though, Hindemith's influence as a composer has not been as significant as his huge output and educational theories might lead one to believe, though the respect he enjoys amongst musicians is indisputable.

Shostakovich

If only in terms of quantity, Dmitri Shostakovich (1906–1975) could be described as the last of the great symphonists, a composer building a career from this genre. In terms of quality, there is an epic breadth matched by few other twentieth century symphonists. His symphonies span a creative life and, like Mahler, whose symphonic vision influenced him, his popularity grew apace in the final years of his own century, somewhat more than Prokofiev. Millennium audiences have empathized with Mahler's massive works, with their tragedy, heroism and pathos, and their suggested autobiographical hints. Likewise with Shostakovich, a composer writing under grim and oppressive Stalinist totalitarianism.

Shostakovich was a prolific composer, and apart from the symphonies, there is a wealth of other orchestral music, including concertos for piano, violin and cello, much of it frequently performed. Stylistically, he did not engage with modernism and experimentation to the same extent as the more cosmopolitan Prokofiev. Nonetheless, in their use of twentieth century tonal language, and their adaptation of classical genres and forms, these composers share similarities of style. Not to underestimate in any way the important concertos, it is the symphonies which capture the essence of Shostakovich, and which will be concentrated on below.

Despite the nationalistic titles of some of Shostakovich's symphonies, he was under no illusions about how the politics of the Soviet Union stifled creativity. The way in which his *Fourth Symphony in C minor* (1936), and *Fifth Symphony in D minor* (1937) became caught up in the politics of the day, has become something of a *cause célèbre* in the annals of twentieth century music. In January 1936, the Soviet daily newspaper *Pravda* issued a blistering editorial attack on Shostakovich's new opera *Lady Macbeth of Mtsensk*. It was also an attack on modernism in general, and on what was perceived to be *bourgeois,* or 'formalist', art, as opposed to that which should come under the banner of Socialist Realism.

Musical folklore tells us that Shostakovich felt it prudent to withdraw his *Fourth Symphony*, and to review his compositional options. That Stalin was behind the *Pravda* editorial seems likely, and it is well known that many artists and members of the intelligentsia were killed or disappeared if they lost favor in Stalin's eyes. In reality, it is uncertain whether the editorial precipitated the withdrawal of the *Fourth Symphony*, but the fact remains that it did not see the light of day again, after some revisions, until 1961. Whatever the real reasons for the work's withdrawal, what followed, the *Fifth Symphony*, was described by the composer as "An artist's reply to just criticism". It seems unlikely, of course, that Shostakovich felt *Pravda's* criticisms to be just, though with the new symphony, Shostakovich's flirtations with the modernism of his earlier works seem to be over for good.

The *Second Symphony, October* (1927), and *Third Symphony, May Day* (1929) are more akin to choral odes than symphonies. There is nothing in these works which matches the originality and invention of the *First Symphony in F minor* (1925), and whereas the youthfulness of this work has endeared it to audiences, its following two symphonies remain curios.

However, there can be no doubting the popularity and quality of the *Fifth Symphony*, one of the most well-liked of twentieth century works within its genre. The *Fifth* is entirely orchestral, and cast in a more or less conventional four movement symphonic scheme, complete with a tautly argued first movement, followed by a dance-like movement complete with trio section, then a true slow movement, and topped by a triumphal finale. It contains some of Shostakovich's finest music, and although he later matched it, he rarely surpassed it.

The influences of Mahler and Tchaikovsky are never too far away in this symphony, though this does not suggest any unoriginality on Shostakovich's part. Rather, it demonstrates that he was able to assimilate their compositional procedures and gestures to create something original. The slow movement, one of the greatest in all symphonic literature, is truly Beethovenian in emotional and structural breadth. Any criticism levelled at the finale might be due to its jubilation sounding, at the end, somewhat forced or hollow. In truth, the finale's, and indeed the whole symphony's, move from minor to major, from darkness to light, is skilful, and an effective assimilation of similar devices found in Beethoven's *Fifth Symphony* or works by Mahler. There is in fact a suggestion, from Shostakovich himself in his posthumously published dictated memoirs, that the final bars of the *Fifth Symphony*, complete with thumping bass drum, is an image of the State drumming into its citizens the edict to be happy.

The shorter, *Sixth Symphony in B minor* (1939) is novel for its opening slow movement followed by two very fast movements, the finale having a sense of jollity which is largely absent in the earlier symphonies. The *Seventh Symphony in C, Leningrad* (1941), and the *Eighth Symphony in C minor* (1943), are what have become known as the War Symphonies. The *Leningrad* was composed when that city was besieged by the Nazis, and became immensely popular, not least because of the huge march in the first movement, said to evoke the approaching German army. Anything sinister, though, is achieved not so much by what is, in fact, quite a jaunty tune, but by a gradual buildup of tension and noise, calculated in a way not dissimilar to Ravel's *Bolero* of some ten years previous. As an orchestral *tour de force*, it has its moments; as a terrifying vision of war, it hardly works. Bartók noted the banality of the material when he parodied it in the fourth movement of his *Concerto for Orchestra*.

The *Eighth Symphony* is tighter, with strongly defined and memorably dark material. The emotional exhaustion one feels at the end of the *Fifth Symphony's* slow movement is, in the *Eighth*, all pervasive. When, in his memoirs, Shostakovich describes his symphonies as 'tombstones', this conjures up the magnificent monolith that is the *Eighth*.

Perhaps Shostakovich's real ninth symphony is the *Tenth Symphony in E minor* (1953). Like the *Fifth* and *Eighth*, this is a large work, considered by many to be the finest of the set, and incorporating, most notably in the fourth movement, Shostakovich's frequently used musical autograph: DSCH (D, E flat, C and B). The *Ninth Symphony in E flat* (1945) on the other hand, belies its traditional numerical associations, as here we have his most classically conceived symphony, relatively short and, by Shostakovich's standards, employing a modestly sized orchestra. The *Eleventh Symphony in G minor, The Year 1905* (1957), and the *Twelfth in D minor, The Year 1917* (1961) are, as the titles suggest, programmatic. By this time, though, the achievements of some of the previous symphonies outshine these two works.

With the *Thirteenth Symphony in B flat minor, Babi Yar* (1962), Shostakovich courted political controversy once more. The work's title takes its name from the first movement, a setting of Yevgeny Yevtushenko's (b. 1933) poem. This speaks out against the government's failure to afford any recognition to Jewish martyrdom when, in 1941, the German SS massacred thirty-four thousand Jews at the Babi Yar ravine near Kiev. The symphony created a storm, despite the so-called post-Stalinist cultural thaw, and the texts had to be censored. The work's premiere turned into a form of anti-government demonstration, and future performances were banned.

Shostakovich went on to compose two further symphonies, by which time his position as a major twentieth century composer was secure. With prolificacy, however, occasionally comes a certain amount of routineness. At its worst, then, there are those moments in his music where well-used and trusted techniques are employed. These include bars of repetitive rhythmic ideas which become formulaic at best, and which lapse into note-spinning at worst, allowing the composer to write an abundance of music in a short space of time. At his finest, Shostakovich produced some of the most excellent and memorable orchestral works of the century.

Gershwin and the American Dream

Compared to the European tradition, the history of concert music in the USA is a short one, but no less exciting because of that. For one thing, the USA is the birthplace of jazz, here used as a generic term to include all those other non-classical styles associated with it. By the end of the nineteenth century, the USA, and New York in particular, already had a thriving classical music scene. In fact, far earlier, Haydn and Beethoven had music performed in New York during their lifetimes. By 1842, the New York Philharmonic had been established. The Juilliard School of Music was founded in that city in 1905, Dvořák worked in New York between 1892 and 1895, and Mahler first conducted at the Metropolitan Opera in 1908.

By 1916, one of the USA's most experimental composers, Henry Cowell (1897–1965) – with whom Gershwin briefly studied – was pushing at the frontiers of musical language with cluster tones – chords made up, literally, of fistfuls of notes. Long before then, in the 1850s, the songwriter Stephen Foster (1826–1864), often cited as America's first national composer, had written *Camptown Races, Swanee River, Old Folks at Home, My Old Kentucky Home* and *Jeanie with the Light Brown Hair*. By the late 1890s, Scott Joplin (1867 or 1868–1917) was writing piano rags, and Edward MacDowell (1860–1908) had produced a number of orchestral works. So, by the time Charles Ives was composing, he was not writing in some sort of musical vacuum, because there was already this strong musical tradition, with its own established infrastructure. And yet, he is the only American composer whose orchestral works from the earliest years of the twentieth century are still regularly performed today. To put the newness of American music in context, all the composers discussed below lived within recent memory. Gershwin, for example, was only just born in the nineteenth century.

Not only American music history, but world music history was made in New York's Aeolian Hall in 1924, and that occasion had not been arrived at by chance. It was part of an exciting musical continuum which was as bold as anything happening in mainland Europe. That event was the premiere, on 12th February, of Gershwin's *Rhapsody in Blue*. George Gershwin (1898–1937), the classically trained composer and pianist, at home writing and performing jazz, Broadway and concert works, wanted to make jazz – here cited generically to include elements such as ragtime and blues – as respectable and as serious as classical music.

He wanted his meld of jazz and classical to challenge the listener in the same way that classical music can, and not be mere popular entertainment as some jazz was prone to be. He was assisted in his quest by the bandleader Paul Whiteman who, in the previous year, staged a concert which presented a fusion of classical and jazz. The 1924 concert, however, advertised as 'An experiement in Jazz', was far more ambitious. The idea to perform jazz, which has improvisation as its base, in such a formal setting, was daring. So he commissioned Gershwin to compose *Rhapsody in Blue* for piano and jazz band – to formally notate improvisatory-like music, and to marry a title borrowed from, say, Liszt or Brahms, with a term never used in classical music – Blue.

Gershwin was not, of course, the first composer to incorporate jazz into classical forms. Examples from Stravinsky, Ravel, Milhaud and others predate *Rhapsody in Blue*. But Gershwin's aesthetic was different from these composers. He wanted to assimilate jazz idioms into concert music, rather than insert, or graft on, this style. It is interesting to note that so many American composers, as we shall see, have one specific iconic piece. In Gershwin's case, as far as his concert music is concerned, it has to be *Rhapsody in Blue*, a title so associated with that composer, that as early as 1945, a biopic about him carried that selfsame title.

The original scoring of the *Rhapsody* was for piano and large jazz band, though the version most familiar with audiences is the 1942 orchestration by the talented arranger and composer Ferde Grofé (1892–1972), himself the creator of the admired *Grand Canyon Suite* (1931). The original version for band, however, is now sometimes performed. There are compositional weaknesses with the *Rhapsody*, in part due to Gershwin's inexperience at handling large-scale form, and in part due to its rapid composition.

Structurally, it may show Lisztian influences, but in truth, there is not the same structural unity as in the later orchestral works. That the *Rhapsody* is largely just a string of memorable melodies with impressive piano writing, and a big tune to round it off, has not worked to its disadvantage. Despite the weaknesses, Gershwin did a daring thing, and for that reason alone it marks a watershed in twentieth century music.

There is, perhaps, a sense of struggle with Gershwin's concert works, which is never evident in the Broadway musicals and songs which enjoy a wonderful feeling of fluency. Maybe this struggle has something to do with the marriage of what one might call art music on the one hand, and popular music on the other hand, and Gershwin's aspiration for his concert works to be taken seriously. With each subsequent concert work, there is an incremental increase in mastery of form and orchestration, and in the ability to sustain long periods of classically developed material.

This evolution can be traced from the *Rhapsody* of 1924, to his first purely orchestral work, *An American in Paris* (1928), and finally to that undisputed, wondrous opera *Porgy and Bess* (1935). Just one year after the *Rhapsody*, Gershwin composed the *Piano Concerto in F* (1925). He had learned, from the *Rhapsody's* deficiencies, how to manage his material in a more succinct way. For example, the Charleston-like figure of the first movement seems to integrate itself comfortably within a sonata form structure. The integration of jazz and classical elements are here more fluent, and the orchestration is, this time, his own.

Gershwin was an experimenter. Had he lived beyond his thirty-six years, we can only speculate what direction his music would have taken. He died a world famous millionaire, a rarity amongst classical composers. His influence was hugely significant, and he taught the next generation that classical and popular styles can inhabit the same world. Had Brahms, Dvořák, Tchaikovksy, Elgar – to name just a few – died at the age of thirty-six, their names would have been mere footnotes in our history books.

The musical milieu in America encouraged composers to think in far broader terms about style than their European counterparts. Ives, as we have seen, is difficult to pigeonhole stylistically. Gershwin's music works as well in Carnegie Hall or the Metropolitan Opera as it does on Broadway or in Hollywood. There were other near-contemporaries of Gershwin who likewise flitted easily from the classical to the popular, including Victor Herbert (1859–1924), Wallingford Riegger (1885–1961), Vernon Duke (1903–1969, born Vladimir Dukelsky), and William Grant Still (1895–1978), the author of some five symphonies.

Even the Broadway musical composer Richard Rogers (1902–1979) ventured into the 'serious' orchestral field with the ballet *Slaughter on Tenth Avenue* (1936) and the music for the television documentary *Victory at Sea* (1952), orchestrated by the eminent Broadway and Hollywood arranger Robert Russell Bennett (1894–1981). Others left Europe as classical composers, and arrived in the USA, seeking sanctuary from the Nazis, with an about-turn of style as Hollywood beckoned. Weill has already been mentioned, and to him can be added Erich Korngold (1897–1957), a one-time child prodigy admired by Mahler.

Copland, Carter, Barber and Bernstein

By the middle years of the twentieth century, the USA had a well-established contemporary music network, supported by world eminent composers, and post-school music education institutions to rival any in Europe. The fusion of styles that we have so far observed became an end in itself, rather than a means to an end, for many American composers, something which was not being replicated to any large extent in Europe. Aaron Copland (1900–1990), Elliott Carter (b.1908), Samuel Barber (1910–1981) and Leonard Bernstein (1918–1990) were essentially of the same generation. Unlike his near contemporary Gershwin, Copland did not have a Broadway or Hollywood career, but had assimilated Gershwin's skill at melding contemporary music with jazz and folk idioms; it simply became an integral part of his style, achieved more fluently than Gershwin. But then, unlike Gershwin, Copland had a long life in which to hone this ability.

This is even more pronounced in Bernstein, for if anyone is worthy to be Gershwin's true successor, then it is he. Bold eclecticism became something of a byword for Bernstein; he makes no apologies for it. Those Mahler, Stravinsky, Bartók, Shostakovich, jazz and blues moments in his symphonies and other orchestral works are not, for Bernstein, copyings of style, but 'style' in its own right. Similarly, the iconic and ground-breaking *West Side Story* (1957), part musical, part opera, part ballet, contains the same type of musical cohesion that one might find, say, in a Puccini opera.

Barber, on the other hand, had little interest in jazz or folk music, depending, instead, almost exclusively on his own perspective of classical forms, and relying on 'absolute', non-programmatic, music. Carter, too, had little need for jazz or popular idioms, instead forging ahead with an intricate anti-Romantic language. As if to underline the didacticism of the composer's role in American society, Copland and Bernstein in particular became well-known as imaginative educators, taking full advantage of radio and television, as well as the printed word, in order to raise awareness of classical music amongst ordinary people. Bernstein's famous Harvard Lectures, for instance, remain supreme examples of popular high quality pedagogy. Carter, too, became a respected teacher. Copland and Bernstein were, like Gershwin, performer-composers, with Bernstein being remembered as one of the great conductors of the twentieth century.

Like Gershwin, whose original name was Jacob Gershowitz, Copland (original name Kaplan) and Bernstein belong to that astonishingly rich tradition of American-Jewish composers. Some of the more plaintive, minor key, melodic lines of Gershwin are possibly influenced by traditional synagogue cantorial melodies. Whereas Mahler, for example, embraced Catholicism in an attempt to assimilate in an anti-Semitic

Vienna, Copland and Bernstein found themselves in a society where being Jewish was no bar to success. Consequently, they were able to allow their ethnicity to directly inform their music, in terms of compositional titles, musical material, or both. This is especially so of Bernstein whose identification with his Jewishness – though not, perhaps, with Judaism as theological expression – and his deep love of the State of Israel, is readily expressed in his compositions and practical music-making, as we shall see.

If *Rhapsody in Blue* has become Gershwin's signature tune, then Copland's *Fanfare for the Common Man* (1942) for brass and percussion, which he also incorporated, now for full orchestra, into the finale of his *Third Symphony* (1946), has become his. The *Fanfare* has grown to be a type of American fanfare template, mimicked countless times by Hollywood composers to suggest the patriotic, and borrowed by various arrangers from The Rolling Stones (the album *Love You Live*, 1977), to its use by television networks to introduce sports programs or advertisements selling insurance.

Along with many prominent composers of his era, Copland studied in Paris with the eminent teacher Nadia Boulanger. Through Boulanger, these young composers met the great and the good in European contemporary music. For example, Stravinsky was a frequent visitor to Boulanger's home. Copland's early music, such as the *Symphony for Organ and Orchestra* (1924, revised 1928 as his *First Symphony*), commissioned by Boulanger, demonstrates his embracing of the contemporary European *avant-garde*.

What is evident in these early orchestral works, then, such as *Music for the Theater* (1925), and the *Piano Concerto* (1927), is Stravinskian neo-classicism plus the rhythmic and melodic inflections of jazz. As the 1930s commenced, Copland's technique became somewhat sparer, in what could be described as, again, a Stravinsky-like cool and objective style, as exemplified in the *Short Symphony* (1933), and *Statements* (1935), six short, somewhat cryptic, character pieces for orchestra.

In effect, then, the 1920s up to the mid 1930s constitute two early Copland styles. From the second half of the 1930s, his third period, which was to sustain him for the rest of his creative life, was launched, and it is the music from this period which is most familiar to audiences.

From his travels to Mexico, he was much influenced by the popular type of music he encountered, as is evident in his well-liked orchestral showpiece *El Salón Mexico* (1936). His jazziest orchestral score is the *Clarinet Concerto* (1948), where the jazz component is underlined by the work's dedicatee, the most famous jazz clarinettist of his age, Benny Goodman. As well as jazz, other elements which began to make appearances in his music were, diversely, Shaker hymns and cowboy tunes. A well-known example of the former is the melody *Simple Gifts*, incorporated in the Martha Graham ballet *Appalachian Spring* (1944). Existing in two versions, the original for chamber orchestra, and an orchestral version, it is considered by many to be Copland's finest score.

The cowboy music prevails in the ballet *Billy the Kid* (1938), and in Copland's most popular orchestral score, the ballet *Rodeo* (1942). Suites from the scores of these cowboy ballets are the versions most often performed in the concert hall, and accessible though these works seem, their sophistication of construction belies their popularity. Extrovert though these works generally are, another orchestral piece offers a more reflective view on Copland's style. This is *Quiet City* (1940) for trumpet, cor anglais and strings, originally scored for a chamber ensemble for a short-lived production of Irwin Shaw's play of the same name. Here is night music, though not the distant sounds across Ives's *Central Park in the Dark*, nor Bartók's darkness, filled with night creatures. Instead, Copland's lonely and evocative night has solitary figures wandering around a big city.

Copland's early forays into Schoenbergian serialism were soon replaced by a diatonic tonal style which sustains almost all his music from the mid-1930s. By absorbing all the different types of music mentioned above, it can be seen that Copland's aim was to find a vernacular American style. It has been copied by many an American composer, signalling that his influence, and what he achieved, should not be underestimated. The transparent and lean harmony, the prevalence of 'open' intervals, such as the fifth, and his widely-spaced scoring, gives his music a particularly spacious feel. Many have suggested that it conjures up the wide open vistas of the USA, and the vertical massiveness of its cities. That he was successful in achieving a truly American vernacular, cannot be doubted. With Copland, American contemporary music came of age.

Like Copland, Carter was a Boulanger disciple. However, in many ways, he is the odd man out in this current group of four composers. Whereas the other three have become as popular as latter-day classical composers can be, and whereas their music is familiar with most music lovers, Carter is somewhat different. For one thing, those who like what they know, and know what they like, will undoubtedly be unfamiliar with Carter's music, and perhaps even with his name. And yet, amongst musicians and composers, he has become one of the most highly regarded of twentieth century American composers, being in the front line of contemporary syntax.

To demonstrate this, Carter's chief claim to fame in this respect, is his development of what is known as 'metrical modulation', where the pulse of one passage is changed imperceptibly into the next. Carter's earlier works were neo-classical in style, and clearly tonal. From the 1950s, with such works as the *Variations for Orchestra* (1955), his music became increasingly complex, embracing an intricate rhythmic and atonal style.

Carter's output is not large. Often cited as one of his most important works, is the *Double Concerto* (1961) for piano, harpsichord and two chamber orchestras. Here, Carter is concerned with reconciling two keyboard instruments which have different performance techniques. The piano is touch-sensitive, whereas the harpsichord is not; the piano produces its sounds by means of hammers striking the strings, whereas the harpsichord's strings are plucked. The contrast here between the two instruments, plus the use of two orchestras, is Carter's twentieth century response to the Baroque concerto grosso, which utilizes clear contrasts between instrumental groups.

There are also, in this work, additional contrasts achieved by means of two large percussion groups in each orchestra. Any semblance to Baroque or Classical concerto form is discarded, however. In its place, is a seven-movement arch shape, with a central middle movement. Similarly, material is not so much developed in the classical sense, but a continuous variation form is used.

The significance of Carter's seminal *Double Concerto*, is that it uses a traditional title, but yet is a reinvention of the form itself. Its credentials include Stravinsky's accolade of it being a masterpiece. Later orchestral works include the three-part *Symphonia: sum fluxae pretium spei* (*I am the Prize of Flowing Hope*, 1996), *Boston Concerto* (2002), the short and witty *Micomicón* (2002), *Dialogues* (2003) for piano and large ensemble, *Three Illusions for Orchestra* (2004), and *Soundings* (2005) for piano and orchestra, demonstrating a late outpouring of large-scale works.

That Copland is now regarded as a twentieth century master, is beyond question. Though his music, and that of Gershwin and Bernstein, has become part of standard repertoire, Samuel Barber's music has been on the ascendancy since his death. By the early 1930s, Barber was already beginning to make a name for himself with such works as the overture *The School for Scandal* (1932). This assured, colorful piece was inspired by Sheridan's comedy, though not intended for specific theatrical production. While only twenty-two at the time, typical Barber fingerprints are already evident, not least the haunting second theme, on oboe, which carries the type of poignancy which was to make his music so identifiable.

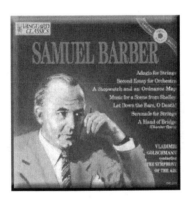

If only for one work, however, Barber's name would be guaranteed: the famous, indeed iconic, *Adagio for Strings* (1936). This work, originally the slow movement from his *String Quartet*, assumed much admired status almost as soon it was premiered under Toscanini. Despite its popularity and its overuse by television documentary makers to tug at viewers' heartstrings, its slow paced, wonderfully controlled unfolding of contemplative and touching material, supported by craftsman-like scoring, makes it a singularly affecting work.

Barber exhibits considerable craftsmanship when handling and sustaining large structures, and manipulating material to support them. The early *School for Scandal* overture demonstrates how well he could utilize sonata form, for example. The two *Essays for Orchestra* (1937 and 1942), often performed together, juxtapose broad themes against small rhythmic and melodic cells. The opening theme of the *Essay No. 1*, for instance, has that now familiar plaintive character, contrasted against the scherzo-like motivic middle section. This same structural care was carried through into the *Second Symphony* (1948).

Other orchestral works have found their way onto the international stage. Most notably, the *Violin Concerto* (1939) belongs with the violin concertos of Berg and Walton as being one of the great lyrical works of this genre from the 1930s. The heartfelt lyricism pervades the first two movements. Indeed, one admires how Barber has two movements which are characterized by overt lyricism, and yet contrast and complement each other. The sonata form of the first movement allows for musical drama, and whilst this drama is not subdued for the second movement, the feeling here is more reflective and nostalgic. It is only in the virtuosic, *perpetuum mobile* of the finale where the character is in marked contrast, as if the sentimentality of the first two movements has been, in effect, exhausted. The other concertos, for cello (1945), piano (1962), and the *Capricorn Concerto* (1944) for flute, oboe, trumpet and strings, do not capture the same intense neo-romantic lyricism as the *Violin Concerto*.

Whereas so many of Barber's contemporaries were forging ahead with daring experimentation, pushing at the boundaries of contemporary compositional language, Barber was content to define his own style. This is characterized by its warm, romantic, tonal idiom, yet always with a strong sense of rhythm and effective orchestration. There is also an indefinable extra with Barber's music. This can be described as artistic integrity, here Barber believing in using quite conventional compositional formulas, some of which were at odds with the *avant-garde* of the day. Interestingly, such is the freshness and honesty of his artistic statements, that his music never seems anachronistic or conservative.

Being something of a musical polymath, one might be forgiven for not knowing quite how to describe Leonard Bernstein's vocation. Many musicians, of course, find themselves composing, performing, conducting, writing and teaching. With Bernstein, though, he excelled, on a world-class scale, in all of these. Hugely energetic, gregarious and fiercely intellectual, he was, by any standards, remarkable. His work as one of the most eminent conductors of his age gave him intimate familiarity with not only the orchestral repertoire but, as a pianist, the chamber repertoire too. That his own music often teems with a diverse and dizzying array of influences, is hardly surprising.

Far more than Copland, who was to influence him and become a close friend, Bernstein's style is difficult to categorize, especially when the stage works are also taken into account. His eclecticism, touched upon above, is reason enough for this. In a sense, this also reflects Bernstein the man, as he, too, refused to be labelled. He was, for example, the father and family man who was also bisexual, the Jew who composed a Mass.

Like Mahler, life and art were one and the same, and for him, life often meant religion and politics. Written during World War II, the *First Symphony, Jeremiah* (1942), for example, in its setting of the ancient text of the prophet, could be said to be about maintaining a belief in God amidst war. This is followed through in the *Third Symphony, Kaddish* (1963), where the narrator talks about man's need for God on the one hand, but also about God's need for man, arguing that if man did not believe, then God would cease to exist. The words, largely by Bernstein himself, but also quoting the ancient Jewish *Kaddish* prayer, again challenge the concept of belief, but conclude by talking about the symbiotic relationship between man and God.

The *Second Symphony, The Age of Anxiety* (1949), is purely instrumental, but is based on W. H. Auden's poem of the same name. Here, the quest is not theological, but a spiritual one, instrumentally argued over by a group of lonely individuals who meet in a New York bar. In terms of form, none of the symphonies approach conventional symphonic structure – whatever that meant by the 1940s. In *The Age of Anxiety*, the bipartite form has as its first movement a set of fourteen variations, and the whole work is, in all but name, a type of piano concerto.

Whether any of the symphonies succeed *as symphonies*, hardly matters, because nobody, and not Bernstein himself, really knew what defined 'symphony' by the 1960s. But they are large-scale orchestral works, where their individual sections are similarly ambitious in structure, and so the word 'symphony' is perhaps more appropriate than any other generic term the composer could have applied. While *The Age of Anxiety* incorporates material which Bernstein later recast into his bluesy pop-song *Ain't Got No Tears Left*, the symphonies are essentially serious, weighty works, though they have not secured their place in the regular symphonic canon.

Of more immediate appeal to audiences, is the bubbly well-known overture to his operetta *Candide* (1956) and, naturally, the *Symphonic Dances* from *West Side Story*. One of his most interesting concert works is the *Prelude, Fugue and Riffs* (1949), for jazz combo, rather than orchestra, and so perhaps not quite within the scope of this book. Here, in a slick and assured way, Baroque technique is effortlessly combined with jazz, plus Stravinskian neo-classicism, recalling Stravinsky's own *Ebony Concerto*.

In the space of twenty-five years, the so-called 'Experiment in modern music' that took place in New York's Aeolian Hall in 1924, had come a long way since *Rhapsody in Blue*, in no small measure due to Copland and Bernstein.

Other Americans born before 1920

It is true that for many concertgoers and music lovers outside of the USA – though the same probably holds true for Americans also – Gershwin, Copland, Bernstein and Barber remain the most well-known of concert composers. But there is a huge amount more, much of it amongst the most exciting, inventive and compelling orchestral music of the twentieth century. However, with such a large number of orchestral works from American composers, any evaluation of the American school has to be, by its very nature, limited.

What follows, is necessarily selective, rather than definitive. In any case, some significant figures did not appreciably contribute to the orchestral repertoire. Cases in point are Marc Blitzstein (1905–1964), Conlon Nancarrow (1912–1997) and George Perle (b.1915).

Although he was born after some of the composers discussed below, pre-eminent amongst the American experimental composers, and one who was to influence a whole generation of composers in the USA and beyond, was John Cage (1912–1992). For many, he is best remembered for his completely silent *4'33"* (1952). For composers, especially in the late 1940s and 1950s, he was something of a guru with regard to aleatoric music, 'chance' music, or music of indeterminacy, as it is often described. Here, chance elements replaced the conventional reliance on rhythm and pitch. This also led Cage to develop graphic scores which did not rely on conventional musical notation. His *Concert for Piano and Orchestra* (1958) does not resemble a piano concerto, even if the title might imply this. The instrumentation is actually for piano and chamber ensemble, rather than orchestra, and there is no score. Instead, there are instrumental parts, and these can be combined in any number of ways. Thus, a performance may include all instruments, or just one, and the duration of the piece is indeterminate.

It follows that if one were looking for a conventional orchestral piece by Cage, then one would be disappointed. Even when the use of an orchestra is cited, this is open to interpretation. For example, in *Branches* (1976), the scoring is for percussion solo, duet, trio or an orchestra of any number of players which includes amplified pods, cacti and other plant materials such as pod rattles from a poinciana tree. As for the duration of the piece, this can be any multiple of eight minutes. While it is unlikely that Cage's music would appear on a program of orchestral music, his influence on twentieth century musical thought was immense.

Though he almost achieved a century, Carl Ruggles (1876–1971) produced relatively few compositions. A friend of Ives, Ruggles's most well-known works were all completed by the 1930s. These include the orchestral pieces *Men and Angels* (1920), *Men and Mountains* (1924) and *Sun-Treader* (1931). At the time, his language was amongst the most progressive and modernist of all the Americans, characterized by being highly chromatic, energetic and, while not strictly serial, largely atonal. Although championed by Ives, Varèse and Cowell, his music struggled during his own lifetime, with *Sun-Treader* not receiving its American premiere until 1966.

Walter Piston (1894–1976) is known by music students the world over for his seminal textbooks on orchestration and harmony. He studied in Paris with Boulanger. As the composer of eight symphonies, plus a well-known ballet score *The Incredible Flutist* (1938), his style is clearly tonal, with traits of European neo-classicism, and a well integrated sprinkling of jazz.

A highly respected composer and music critic, Virgil Thompson (1896–1989), like Piston, was one of the most neo-classical American composers of his generation. He also studied in Paris under Boulanger, and came under the spell of Satie and *Les Six*, which taught him clarity of expression, and economy of musical gesture. Whilst he is best known for his opera *Four Saints in Three Acts* (1928), his relatively small catalog of orchestral works includes the *Concertino, Autumn* (1964) for harp, percussion and strings, and the *Arcadian Songs and Dances* from his Pulitzer Prize film score *Louisiana Story* (1948). Known as much as a conductor as a composer, Howard Hanson (1896–1981) composed seven symphonies, the *Second, Romantic* (1930), has a title which is the key to his style: an unapologetic celebration of the Romantic symphony within a contemporary American setting.

One of the most prolific symphonists of the century, Roy Harris (1898–1979) composed sixteen of them between 1933 and 1979. By the time he was in his thirties, he was, in America, one of the most frequently performed home-grown contemporary composers. Whilst that popularity waned even in his own lifetime, there is little doubt that his *Third Symphony* (1938) is one of the most interesting of American symphonies. It is in one continuous movement, though in five sections, where changes of musical character all take place, rather like Sibelius's *Seventh Symphony*, within a terse and concentrated eithteen minute span. Like so many of his contemporary American composers, Harris's style is overtly tonal and, akin to Copland and Ives, draws upon folk-like music, including cowboy songs, and American congregational hymns. In his own way, and again resembling Ives and Copland, he was contributing to an American vernacular style.

Following in this grand symphonic, tonal idiom, is the music of Harris's pupil William Schuman (1910–1992), the composer of ten symphonies and other large-scale orchestral works. Roger Sessions (1896–1985) also added to the American symphonic tradition by composing eight symphonies (1927–1978), amongst other orchestral works. He studied with Bloch, and though his early work was indebted to him in its Romantic breadth on the one hand, and to Stravinskian neo-classicism on the other hand, he eventually embraced aspects of twelve-tone technique and free atonality, and this range of style is represented in his symphonies.

Sessions was hugely respected by his composer colleagues, and by his students who included Milton Babbitt (see below) and David Diamond (1915–2005). Diamond also studied with Boulanger, and his music was greatly championed by his friend Leonard Bernstein. Like Copland, it is essentially melodic, clearly tonal and, in terms of structure, has neo-classical clarity. He composed eleven symphonies (1940–1993), though his most well-known work is *Rounds* (1944) for string orchestra. The titles of some of his works, like those of Copland and Bernstein, allude to his Jewish heritage. *Kaddish* (1987), for cello and orchestra, has the same title as Bernstein's *Third Symphony*, and is a meditation on this ancient Jewish prayer.

Amongst the most experimental American composers of his generation was George Antheil (1900–1959). With its reliance on jazz, incessantly repeated rhythms, and much noise, his music, certainly in the 1920s, was part of the shock of the new. His *Ballet mécanique* (1925), for example, is scored for eight pianos, pianola, four xylophones, two electric bells, two propellers, tam-tam, four bass drums and siren. The work became something of a *cause célèbre* at its Paris premiere, and for its New York performance in1927, anvils, motor-horns and electric saws were added.

A pioneer of electronic music, Milton Babbitt (b.1916) is noted as being one of the most progressive American composers of his era. Like others who produced their most experimental works after World War II, Babbitt, who studied with Sessions, was keen to develop twelve-tone technique so that all aspects of the music, not just pitch, were serialised and controlled. His purely orchestral works are few, but include *Relata I* (1965) and *Relata II* (1968), whilst *Correspondences* (1967) adds tape to the string orchestra.

Another notable experimenter is Lou Harrison (1917–2003), who studied with innovators such as Cowell and Cage, as well as Schoenberg. His unconventional music follows on from the percussion-writing tradition of the experimentalist Harry Partch (1901–1974). Something of an eclectic composer, Harrison's music shows influences from all over the world, particularly the Far East, though very little from Europe. It puts great emphasis on traditional and non-traditional percussion sounds, including those made by tin cans and flowerpots, though unlike Cage or Varèse, it adheres to clearly defined melodic shapes. Colorful and fascinating works such as *Music for Violin with Various Instruments – European, Asian and African* (1967, revised 1969), or *Threnody for Carlos Chávez* (1978) for viola and gamelan, clearly shows this non-European influence in the way in which the orchestra has been re-defined.

Likewise, the music of Alan Hovhaness (1911–2000) is influenced by oriental and Indian music, using the sounds and instruments from those cultures. Something of a mystic, his large output looks ahead to the music of Arvo Pärt and John Tavener (see below), and includes over sixty symphonies. By contrast, composers such as Leroy Anderson (1908–1975), Morton Gould (1913–1996), and Vincent Persichetti (1915–1987), composed in an overtly tonal and highly accessible style.

Many of Anderson's light, orchestral works, such as *The Typewriter* (1950) and *Sleigh Ride* (1948) fall into the realm of 'easy listening', whilst Gould's music is characterized by brilliant orchestration.

Other Americans born after 1920

As new sounds and compositional procedures encouraged composers to re-think the definition of 'orchestra', it should not surprise us that some significant composers, active post-World War II, should discard the standard orchestra in favor of new groupings of instruments. We have seen this already with composers such as Harrison or Partch. With composers born after 1920, some have sizeable catalogs, though not necessarily with any standard orchestral content. Such composers include the French-born Christian Wolff (b.1934) and La Monte Young (b.1935), where scoring is frequently for unspecified instruments, and Morton Feldman (1926–1987), whose long compositions are often for unusual groups of instruments.

The American symphonic tradition continues with the later generation. For example, the prolific writer/composer Ned Rorem (b.1923), though chiefly admired for his vocal music, has composed three symphonies. Particularly popular with audiences, John Corigliano (b.1938) has written extensively for orchestra, in a style which is tonal and approachable, yet demonstrating structural rigor and organic growth. He has composed two symphonies (1988 and 2000), the *Second* for string orchestra, a *Violin Concerto, The Red Violin* (2003), plus companion pieces *The Red Violin: Suite for Violin and Orchestra* (1999), and *The Red Violin: Chaconne for Violin and Orchestra* (1997).

George Crumb (b.1929), on the other hand, though regarded as one of the most fascinating and inventive American composers of his generation, has written few purely orchestral works. His most well-known one, however, is *Echoes of Time and the River (Echoes II) – Four Processionals* (1967). The work exploits Crumb's preoccupation with time. For example, the players may, if they wish, actually process around the stage in steps of varying length which synchronize with the music. This theatrical and visual aspect, which can also be found in other works, is likewise carried over to the instrumentation. Here, string and wind play antique cymbals and glockenspiel plates, and string players are expected to recite nonsense words.

A highly experimental composer who wrote a small number of orchestral works, Earle Brown (1926–2002) used various types of unconventional musical notation, such as graphic scores, and his music is influenced by contemporary American artists such as Jackson Pollock. German born, though moving to the USA in 1937, Lukas Foss (b.1922) has had a distinguished career as a conductor, pianist, teacher – he was Schoenberg's successor at UCLA – as well as a composer. Like Copland, Bernstein and Diamond, some of Foss's music is informed by his Jewish roots, as in, for example, the *Elegy for Anne Frank* (1989) for piano and orchestra. His earlier works are neo-classical in approach, economical and concise of language, something no doubt learned from his teacher, Hindemith. Later, in such orchestral works as the *Baroque Variations* (1967), where he deconstructs music of the Baroque masters, he adopted twelve-tone technique. Ultimately, his music demonstrates an eclectic approach, especially in later works, for instance the *Renaissance Concerto* (1985) for flute and orchestra.

Post-War Experimental Pioneers

As World War II ended, European music was ready to be taken into the next generation by a group of seminal experimental composers. By 1946, Schoenberg, no longer in mainland Europe, had completed his major works, his pupils Berg and Webern were dead, and twelve-tone technique was well established. Stravinsky was already a senior citizen, and Bartók was dead. In that same year, the International Summer Courses for New Music were inaugurated in Darmstadt, Germany. Students included those who were to be in the vanguard of the *avant-garde* in the 1950s and 1960s: the Italians Bruno Maderna (1920–1973) and Luigi Nono (1924–1990), and the Germans Hans Werner Henze (b.1926), and Karlheinz Stockhausen (1928–2007). Teachers included Messiaen and, in 1953, Stockhausen. By the mid 1950s, the German-American composer Stefan Wolpe (1902–1972), the Italian Luciano Berio (1925–2003), the Frenchmen Pierre Boulez (b.1925) and Henri Pousseur (b.1929) and, most significantly, Cage, were teaching there. Towards the late 1950s, former students Maderna and Nono were teachers. In the 1960s and 1970s, the Argentinian born composer and film-maker Mauricio Kagel (b.1931) taught there.

These people became some of the most significant musicians of the contemporary music scene in the second half of the twentieth century. It is true that some of these figures are mere names for many concertgoers, without any of their music being familiar. This is especially true, for example, of composers such as Pousseur or Nono, whose orchestral music is scant, and generally unfamiliar to symphony audiences. Pousseur's use of aleatory form – in its broadest sense 'chance' music – and Nono's densely packed, at times electronically enhanced, textures, did not lend themselves readily to the symphony orchestra.

Others were preoccupied with integrating music with different art forms. Kagel, for instance, creates surreal works using kaleidoscope or collage techniques, his music being a theatrical collection of disparate snatches and instruments. He is, perhaps, the musical equivalent of, say, Samuel Beckett, engaging in latter-day Dada. In his aesthetic approach, he is close to the German Bernd Alois Zimmerman (1918–1970), who also used collage-type effects. For example, his orchestral piece *Musique pour les soupers du Roi Ubu* (1966) is entirely made up of quotations of music from the Renaissance to the Romantic. As part of this theatrical tradition, Heinz Karl Gruber (b.1943), infamously known for his widely performed music-theater piece *Frankenstein!!* (1977), achieves the theatrical and bizarre in other works such as the *Cello Concerto* (1989), and the *Trumpet Concerto, Aerial* (1999).

Though other composers of the Darmstadt School, not least Henze, would have theatrical elements as part of their works, Berio is perhaps the most gestural of these composers, incorporating an Italian sense of theater in so many of his works. He has become one of the most frequently performed of the Darmstadt composers, due to a more colloquial language which is not always reliant on serialism. His music, however, embraces those aspects common to his Darmstadt contemporaries: serialism (when required); electronics; aleatory music; collage-type techniques. His several *Sequenzas* for solo instruments are now firmly part of the chamber music canon, bringing his name to the direct attention of performers and the wider audience.

Berio's one-time wife was the singer Cathy Berberian (1925–1983), one of the most imaginative vocalists of her age, and herself a composer, who further championed his music on the world stage. *Requies* (1985) for chamber orchestra was written as a memorial for her, though the marriage had been dissolved some years earlier. Not surprisingly, much of Berio's output includes music for voice. For example, the seminal *Sinfonia* (1968) for voices and orchestra, and many chamber works, fall outside the scope of this book. His purely orchestral works include the early *Concertino* (1949), *Nones* (1954), *Variazioni* (1954), *Allelujah I* and *II* (1955, 1957), and the *Concerto for Two Pianos and Orchestra* (1973).

In 1977, Boulez became director of the electronic music studio Institut de Recherche et de Coordination Acoustique/Musique (IRCAM) in Paris. Soon after, he commenced one of his most significant orchestral works, *Répons* (1984), which challenges where we experience musical performances. For it, the composer asks for a square auditorium with removable seating so that the orchestra can be positioned on a raised platform in the middle of it, the keyboard and percussion soloists placed in a circle on platforms against the outer wall, the conductor, live electronics and computer in front of the main orchestra, and the audience in a circle between that and the soloists.

In his most experimental works, Boulez has pushed at the boundaries of *avant-garde* language. Yet, for all the challenges which Boulez's post-Webern total serialism offers, there is a refined delicacy to much of his sound-world, perhaps underlining his Gallic musical tradition. Though being at the forefront of modern music, Boulez has become far more of an establishment figure than, say, Stockhausen, not least because he is also an international conductor, having had prestigious principal conductorships of the New York Philharmonic and BBC Symphony orchestras.

With Stockhausen, however, his notoriety went before his music. If any composer could be labelled the *enfant terrible* of the post-war composers, then it is he. He stood for all that was shocking and modern, with many people disliking his music without ever having heard a note of it. In his most oft-cited orchestral work, *Gruppen* (*Groups*, 1957), three orchestras are placed around the audience, each with its own conductor.

Material is passed from one orchestra to the other, in effect commented on as it proceeds on its transformational journey. The aural effect is stunning, yet the musical experience is demanding in the way in which Stockhausen, like others of the Darmstadt School, serialized not just (as with Schoenberg) pitch, but durations (ie, rhythm) also. Boulez and Messiaen, for example, totally serialized more or less all aspects of the sound.

Exciting and daring as *Gruppen* is, inevitably works such as this will rarely win the hearts of subscription concert audiences. If they still resist the Second Viennese School, after almost one hundred years, some music of the Darmstadt composers will have an uphill struggle to find acceptance. In truth, this is a pity, for works such as *Gruppen*, or Stockhausen's *Mixtur* (1964), for orchestra and electronics, represent all that is exciting in experimental, risk-taking music of the period. One does not need to understand the theory behind the sounds in order to take pleasure in the aural experience. What Stockhausen and the other Darmstadt composers, especially Boulez, Pousseur and Nono, were doing, was pushing at the frontiers of received wisdom of musical language.

The same is true of their other contemporaries, such as the Greek composer Iannis Xenakis (1922–2001), whose works are preoccupied with the relationship between music, mathematics and probability, somewhat informed by his early training as an engineer. He produced what he described as 'stochastic' music, involving or containing a random variable or variables. Xenakis's music is, not surprisingly, immensely complex in terms of theory, texture, performance and notation. In the orchestral music, such as *Metastaseis* (1954) for sixty-five musicians, we find a sound-mass technique of dense, yet sonorous, textures, comprising string parts preoccupied with multiple glissandos, and with many disparate sounds happening simultaneously.

In fact, these composers were so cutting-edge, producing completely novel sounds in the 1950s and 1960s, that there was a huge test amongst the next generation to produce something fresh and untried. Quite often, though with a few exceptions, those who were intent in trying to replicate the audacity of the *avant-garde* of the 1950s and 1960s, failed. Several composers, such as Peter Maxwell Davies or Arvo Pärt, did not even try, but instead struck out in new directions, as we shall see. Some, such as the British composer Brian Ferneyhough (b.1943), himself becoming a Darmstadt teacher in the 1970s, integrated and expanded contemporary experimentations. His complex and virtuosic orchestral work *Firecycle Beta* (1971) is testament to this. Others embraced a new Romanticism, ideally suited to the tried and tested symphony orchestra. These include British composers Nicholas Maw (b.1935), Robin Holloway (b.1943), typically in his *Violin Concerto* (1990), James MacMillan (b.1959), discussed later on or, as previously cited, John Corigliano.

Still others represented a more conservative, though by no means less 'modern', strand amongst the Darmstadt composers and their contemporaries. A case in point is Henze. By the time of his Darmstadt days, he had moved from his Stravinsky-Hindemith influenced period, into writing twelve-tone music. By the mid 1950s, however, he had split with the mainstream *avant-garde*, composing music where melody and lyricism was all-important. Henze has composed ten symphonies (1947–2000), and he is undoubtedly one of the most significant of post-World War II symphonists, though his vocal/operatic output is perhaps his most considerable area. To underline the lyrical aspect, the *Eighth Symphony* (1993) has been described by the composer as "a summer piece", inspired by, though not describing, Shakespeare's *A Midsummer Night's Dream*.

Not all his works, however, have such uncontroversial influences. His *Sixth Symphony* (1969), for example, was written at the height of his infatuation with left-wing politics, and includes quotes from Vietnamese and Greek liberation songs. His *Second Violin Concerto* (1971), one of more than twenty concertos, has a subtext, too, this time of the artist, represented by the violinist, retaining his independence and integrity within society at large. It is a semi-theater piece, with the soloist (or narrator) expected to narrate an electronically distorted version of Hans Magnus Enzensberger's poem *Hommage à Gödel*.

Lutosławski, Ligeti, Penderecki, and others born before 1950

We have already seen in the music of the Darmstadt School, and in Cage and others, how indeterminacy/aleatoric/chance music has been employed. The Polish composer Witold Lutosławski (1913–1994) engineered his own type of aleatoric music, with its own notation. Whilst he was keen to push ahead with innovatory notation which would support those aleatoric passages, his sound-world is essentially accessible. There are passages in his music where the harmony suggests atonality, but also places of harmonic tension and release, just as there is in conventional tonal music.

Evident, too, are passages where folk-like themes offer contrast against dense chromaticism. In fact, in his *Concerto for Orchestra* (1954), which is one of his most frequently performed works, there is an abundance of diatonic, folk-like material. The work is, in effect, a tribute to Bartók and, in particular, his *Concerto for Orchestra* – at that time only a decade old – demonstrating Lutosławski's indebtedness to the great Hungarian. The same is true of *Funeral Music* (1958) for strings. Written to commemorate the tenth anniversary of Bartók's death, though completed somewhat late, it uses the first movement of Bartók's *Music for Strings, Percussion and Celeste* as its model. It is also the only work by Lutosławski to employ a tone row, though one which is not used strictly serially.

It was in 1960 that Lutosławski first heard Cage's *Concerto for Piano*. It was not so much Cage's application of 'prepared' piano which so intrigued Lutosławski, but rather Cage's use of indeterminacy. It gave rise to the first work where Lutosławski employs aleatoric techniques, *Jeux Vénitiens* (*Venetian Games*, 1961) for small orchestra. From this work onwards Lutosławski's use of aleatoricism typically allows for instruments to improvise around a motive of pitches, though not veering from the notes themselves, and according to their own rhythm and speed. This might be employed either for individual instruments, or for groups. Sometimes, note values are specified, but only to be observed to an extent.

The underlying idea behind all of this, of course, is that synchronization between players should only be approximate. The conductor indicates, with cues, when performers should move on to the next section. But because each instrumentalist has their own notated part, though one which is performed with artistic licence, different performances of the same piece will be similar, unlike with some other 'chance' pieces where each performance is almost like a new work. This system became central to his style, yet later works such as the *Piano Concerto* (1988) and *Fourth Symphony* (1992) rely far more on conventional notation.

Lutosławski composed four symphonies. In addition to the *Piano Concerto*, there is a *Cello Concerto* (1970), and a *Double Concerto* (1980) for oboe and harp. Other significant orchestral works include *Livre pour orchestre* (1968), *Mi-Parti* (1976), *Chain 3* (1986) and the 1978 arrangement for piano and orchestra of the two-piano *Variations on a Theme by Paganini* (1941).

Another noteworthy, but relatively neglected, Polish composer is Andrzej Panufnik (1914–1991). This neglect is possibly due, in part, to his pre-1945 works having been lost during the Nazi occupation of Poland, in part Panufnik's difficulty in the 1950s, due to McCarthyism, in traveling and working in the USA, and in part due to an unofficial BBC ban on his music in the 1970s, when the European *avant-garde* was favored above some of the more conventional home-grown music. Panufnik settled in the UK in 1954 where he composed his most significant works. These embrace seven of his ten symphonies, and a large amount of orchestral music, including concertos for violin (1971), bassoon (1985) and cello (1991). His music is characterized by its solemn and at times spiritual language, using, like Lutosławski, aleatoric techniques. There is a directness of chromatic, yet tonal, language which in many ways makes it as accessible, if not more so, as Lutosławski's music. Panufnik's daughter, Roxanna Panufnik (b.1968), has followed in her father's footsteps, and is one of the UK's leading younger generation composers.

Poland became, in the latter years of the twentieth century, a progressive place for contemporary music. Significant here is Krzysztof Penderecki (b.1933). Still in his twenties, he was rocketed to fame on the *avant-garde* scene with his *Threnody for the Victims of Hiroshima* (1960) for fifty-two strings. Influenced by sound-mass, Xanakis-type sonority, the musical theory behind the notes is one of texture, rather than melody, harmony, rhythm, or motives. Vertical harmony is replaced with dense note-clusters, supported by extended string technique. The work's intensity, indeed the expressiveness that the texture gives rise to, underscores the harrowing and emotional connotations of the work's title.

By the 1970s, the bold experimentation in Penderecki's earlier works had been replaced with, surprisingly, a type of neo-romanticism. The *Violin Concerto* (1974), for example, shows little evidence of the sound-mass composer of the 1960s. And his *Christmas Symphony* (1980) – one of eight symphonies – uses the carol *Silent Night* as its starting point. Even so, the textures of his earlier works were not entirely abandoned, as is testament in some of the later pieces. However, the ease with which Penderecki has been able to replace daring experimentalism with tonal chromaticism, demonstrates the unquestionable mastery and confidence of this composer.

Along with Penderecki, Henryk Górecki (b.1933) was the leading Polish experimenter of that generation. Preoccupied with texture and sonority, he moved from a neo-classical early style to one which employed twelve-tone technique. Unexpectedly, though, he is remembered for none of this, but instead for his *Third Symphony, The Symphony of Sorrowful Songs* (1976). Undoubtedly one of the most popular classical works of the final quarter of the twentieth century, its static, diatonic language aptly supports the words which lament a mother's loss for her Gestapo-imprisoned son, echoing the loss experienced by Jesus's mother. Though a vocal work, it is indicative of Górecki's later style, and of a significant composer brought to international fame by just one composition.

The idea of sound-mass, as exemplified in the orchestral works of Penderecki or Xenakis, is a defining feature of the music of Hungarian born György Ligeti (1923–2006). His music was brought to public attention when *Atmosphères* (1961) was used in Kubrick's film *2001: A Space Odyssey*. Not only is it appropriately filmic to suggest deep space, but this work is typical of the orchestral textural aspects of Ligeti's music. Though for full orchestra, Ligeti stipulates the number of strings to be employed. These are not used as a traditional 'choir' of strings, but rather twenty-eight individual violins, ten violas, ten cellos and eight double basses. Though compositionally the contrapuntal device of canon is employed, this is only a means to an end, the end being a thick web of sound. In any case, though the canonic devices are visual on the page, they are impossible to locate aurally.

The same effects are observed and heard in other orchestral works, too, such as the earlier *Apparitions* (1959). Any rhythmic changes are imperceptible, allowing the textures to float outside of time, and with no sense whatsoever of a pulse or tempo. Ligeti himself described his type of sound-mass as 'micropolyphony'. During the 1970s, as his music placed less reliance on dense chromaticism, it became more preoccupied with rhythm. Used in such a way, it resembled the rhythmic features that would become the mainstay of the American minimalists. Ligeti's last orchestral work was the *Hamburg Concerto* (1999, revised 2003) for solo horn and chamber orchestra with four obligato natural horns, and it confirms that, right up to the end, Ligeti was undoubtedly the most inventive Hungarian composer since Bartók.

The attempts by composers such as Ligeti to suspend the temporal aspect of music, is a fascinating feature of the *avant-garde* from the 1950s onwards. There are antecedents in earlier works, too, such as Messiaen's *Quartet for the End of Time* (1941), the later works of Webern (1930s and 1940s) or even, it could be argued, the slow movement from Beethoven's *A minor String Quartet* (1825). In a more simplistic way than works from the 1950s or 1960s, other composers began to write music which was at times largely static. Here, rhythmic, melodic and harmonic ideas would be kept to a minimum, allowing the music to unfold very slowly in an almost hypnotic manner, and offering a wash of sound, rather than clearly defined events.

A well known example of this, a work which has won the hearts of audiences world-wide, is the *Cantus in memoriam Benjamin Britten* (1977) for string orchestra and bell, by the Estonian Arvo Pärt (b.1935).

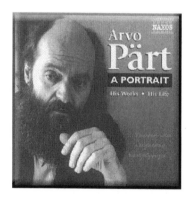

With Pärt, as we shall now see with others, we leave the bold experiments of many of the composers discussed above, and enter a simpler world, one which is influenced by religion and ceremony. Pärt embraced the Russian Orthodox Church in the 1970s, after a period where his music was informed by such diverse sources as Schoenberg, Bartók and Shostakovich. With his religious revelation, came his study of plainchant and Renaissance polyphony.

The works with which he is now most familiar to us, all date from the 1970s onwards, and are preoccupied, to some extent, with bell sounds. Pärt calls this 'tintinnabuli' – literally, the ringing of bells. His music is harmonically simple, often based on just one diatonic chord which seldom changes or moves, and which offers no room for modulation. The rhythms are similarly simple. *Cantus in memoriam Benjamin Britten* serves well to demonstrate this, with the solo bell punctuating the texture and adding a slight sense of discord against the diatonic strings. These features also currently maintain his style, in later works such as *Lamentate* (2003) for piano and orchestra, and the orchestral *La Tela Traslata* (2006).

The British composer John Tavener (b.1944) also embraced Russian Orthodoxy. Like Pärt with his *Cantus in memoriam Benjamin Britten*, and Górecki with his *Symphony of Sorrowful Songs*, Tavener's music has reached a wide audience. His work for cello and strings, *The Protecting Veil* (1988), enjoyed immense popularity soon after it was premiered at the 1989 BBC Proms in London. It received numerous subsequent live performances, and went into the CD charts when the recording was issued. It now boasts a number of recordings in the CD catalog. His popularity was further enhanced by the inclusion of *Song for Athene* (1993) for the funeral of Diana, Princess of Wales, in 1997.

The Protecting Veil commemorates the Feast of the Protecting Veil, which goes back to 10th century Byzantium. The music is, for the most part, slow and ceremonial, largely diatonic, melodic in a chant-like, vocal way. Chord clusters on strings suggest the sound of bells, rather than the real bells one finds in Pärt. What Tavener has in common with Pärt in particular, is a directness of language, and the composer's affirmation of religious faith through the music. It would seem that this aids the music's popularity, and perhaps, then, post-modernist society is not too godless after all. Certainly, there was not much room for religious fervor during the Darmstadt period, Messiaen excepted.

Similarly less reliant on Darmstadt-related modernism, though not enjoying the popularity of Pärt or Tavener, is the music of composers such as the Russians Sofia Gubaidulina (b.1931) and Alfred Schnittke (1934–1998). Though their brand of serialism was less severe than that of their Western European colleagues, they still fell out of favor with the Soviet authorities.

Gubaidulina draws on Russian folk music and its instruments to help define her style, and this has often resulted in conventional instruments being used in unconventional ways. Her music has the sense of the epic. In *Feast During a Plague* (2005), for example, based on a short scenario by Pushkin, the large orchestra sustains this twenty-five minute span with music which is bleak, apocalyptic, and demandingly dissonant. It is a piece which lays down a marker for orchestral music at the beginning of the new millennium. Similarly, a work such as *The Light at the End* (2003) uses a very big orchestra to create a powerful and massive statement.

Schnittke eventually arrived at what he desribed as 'polystylism' which, as the name suggests, draws on a number of different styles and composers, a type of collage pastiche. This is clearly noticeable in the composition which first brought him to prominence in the West, the *Concerto Grosso No.1* (1977) for two violins, prepared piano, harpsichord and strings. In this, we find an amalgam of Baroque gestures, recalling Corelli and Vivaldi, juxtaposed by highly chromatic language which employs microtones, and popular music.

The later works, such as the *Viola Concerto* (1985), place less reliance on polystylism, and in its place there is a starker, bleaker sound. The opening of the *Sixth Symphony* (1996) is a case in point. It is not difficult to realize why Schnittke is considered the true heir of Shostakovich. Both composers use parody and irony, but there is also an anxiousness in their music, perhaps encouraged by living under an oppressive regime. In Schnittke's case, his final years were also dogged by ill health, eventually leaving him more or less paralyzed. Though he started his *Ninth Symphony* in 1997, it was left unfinished at his death.

Louis Andriessen (b.1939) is regarded as one of the Netherland's most distinguished contemporary composers. He has rarely written for conventional symphony orchestra, instead writing for various instrumental combinations. For example, *De snelheid* (*Velocity*, 1983, revised 1984) uses three orchestras which incorporates Hammond organs, electric keyboards, electric harps, bass guitar, with most of the instruments amplified. *Vermeer Pictures* (2005) for orchestra includes two electric guitars and cimbalom. His music shows influences from jazz to minimalism, via Stravinsky, Ives and medieval music, and incorporating, *en route*, his interests in shipbuilding, atomic science and politics. Poul Ruders (b.1949), on the other hand, regarded as Denmark's leading post-World War II composer, continues to engage with symphonic and concerto forms.

Away from Europe or the USA, Tôru Takemitsu (1930–1996) stands as the most eminent Far Eastern composer whose music has made an impact on the Western scene. His works have an essentially

Western language, but with references to Japanese music and instruments. *Dream/Window* (1985), for example, uses an amplified guitar to suggest the Japanese koto, whilst the piece itself is modelled, in musical terms, on a garden in Kyoto designed by a sixteenth century Zen monk. His *November Steps* (1967), on the other hand, perhaps his most well-known orchestral piece, uses the traditional Japanese instruments of the biwa and shakuhachi.

The Music of Tōru Takemitsu

In the UK, the composers of the so-called Manchester School have had a significant impact on contemporary British music. Alexander Goehr (b.1932), Harrison Birtwistle (b.1934) and Peter Maxwell Davies (b.1934) were all studying together at the then Royal Manchester College of Music in the 1950s, and it is Birtwistle and Maxwell Davies in particular who have helped shape the UK's contemporary music scene. Birtwistle's music has often irked concert audiences, largely because they perceive it as brutal and aggressive. It is true that the violent rhythmic aspect of his work might suggest this, though in essence it is often there to underline the dramatic and theatrical bent to his art. Certainly, his earlier works exhibit the percussive influences from Varèse, and rhythmic aspects of Messiaen. But they also reveal his indebtedness to the theatrical side of

Stravinsky, especially as exemplified in such works as the latter's *Agon* ballet. This theatrical aspect lends itself to Birtwistle's penchant for dividing his music into 'scenes'. In other words, it tends to be episodic, rather than classically organically symphonic. His most important orchestral compositions include *The Triumph of Time* (1971), a processional *tour de force* based on Breughel the Elder's engraving, and the piece which first brought Birtwistle's name onto the orchestral concert platform.

Birtwistle's music undoubtedly makes demands on average subscription concert audiences. When *Panic* (1995) for saxophone, drum-kit and orchestra, was premiered at London's Last Night of the Proms, it was greeted with consternation by audience and critics alike. That contemporary music can provoke such reactions must be a good thing, demonstrating that Birtwistle feels he needs to challenge the listener. Certainly, for those who can be challenged, and for those who can listen to his aural experience, Birtwistle has produced some of the most exciting and thought-provoking contemporary British scores.

Maxwell Davies, in his earlier music, similarly provoked audiences with such works as the iconic music theater chamber piece *Eight Songs for a Mad King* (1969). Unlike Birtwistle, though, there is a popular aspect to his style. Although some of his music relies on serialism, it also uses systems such as numerology and magic squares as starting points to create pitch-sets. Maxwell Davies has also made a detailed study of medieval and Renaissance techniques, and these have directly influenced his own working processes. When Maxwell Davies moved to the remote Orkney Islands off Scotland's north-east coast in the early 1970s, his music began to show influences from Scottish folklore. The *First* and *Second Fantasias on John Taverner's In Nomine* (1962 and 1964), or the monolithic *First Symphony* (1976), are amongst the most modernist and demanding of Maxwell Davies's orchestral pieces. On the other hand, *St. Thomas Wake – Foxtrot for Orchestra on a Pavan by John Bull* (1969), for example, offers a more accessible, though no less rigorously conceived, style. Even more popular are the orchestral pieces *Mavis in Las Vegas* (1997), and *An Orkney Wedding, with Sunrise* (1985), which features solo bagpipes.

His *Eighth*, and by all accounts final symphony, *Antarctic Symphony* (2000), written as a tribute to Vaughan Williams's *Sinfonia Antartica* (1952), places the concept of millennium-style program music in context. When Vaughan Williams composed this work, based on his music from the 1948 film *Scott of the Antarctic*, it would have been inconceivable for him to personally experience the rigors of that icy expanse; the world was still a very big place in the 1940s and 1950s. For Maxwell Davies, however, he traveled to the Antarctic to witness it firsthand. His symphony's opening depicts ice being cracked by the ship that he was actually on, and so when he musically conjures up the vastness and stillness of the region, he is writing from what he saw. In addition to his symphonies, Maxwell Davies, who was appointed Master of the Queen's Music in 2004, has composed a cycle of ten *Strathclyde Concertos* (1986–1996) for various instruments, commissioned by Scotland's Strathclyde Regional Council.

CHAPTER 8

—

Into the Millennium

Styles adjust, tastes change. What was shocking thirty or fifty years ago might today seem passé or simply anachronistic. The bright young thing or *enfant terrible* of yesterday becomes the grand old benighted man or woman of today. And tomorrow? Who knows? Now, in the early years of a new century, the distinction between different musical styles and genres are more blurred than ever. Classical musicians or composers cross over into popular styles. World music, ethno-music, has become mainstream, and the musicians who devote themselves exclusively to 'art music' might well be a dying breed. Some composers have embraced this, and refuse to limit themselves to style, genre or school.

A notable example is the post-minimalist American composer Michael Torke (b.1961). He has his own CD label which has produced all his music, the boxed set of which became one of the top classical albums of 2004. Orchestral works such as *An Italian Straw Hat* (2004) and *Heartland* (2006) demonstrate that to pigeonhole such a composer would be dangerous. Torke is a distinctive example of the classical composer responding to a changing world, and where received notions about 'classical' or 'orchestra' or 'serious composer' or 'art music' are re-assessed.

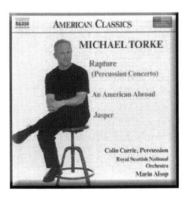

Certainly, with so much accessible classical music available commercially, or even free on the web, it has not resulted in an increase of audience capacity at symphony concerts. Despite the abundance of new music being produced, despite the ease with which today's composers can have their music commercially recorded, orchestral concerts still largely concentrate on the music of dead composers, and most of those within a one hundred and forty year window between the late eighteenth to the early twentieth centuries.

It seems likely that the music of the minimalists might well stand the test of time. Minimalism started as something of an experiment in the 1960s. Today it is considered mainstream, with music by the Americans Steve Reich (b.1936), Terry Riley (b.1936), Philip Glass (b.1937) and John Adams (b.1947) enjoying much popularity. Indeed, if there is a vernacular for classical music written during the last forty years of the twentieth century, history might well cite minimalism as the definer. With its emphasis on simple, often diatonic, harmony, and with its reiteration of short melodic and rhythmic fragments which transform imperceptibly, it is not aurally demanding in the same way that some contemporary music is. Much of it, for example, and rather like pop music, stays on the same emotional plane.

There are today innumerable composers who either use some sort of minimalist, or post-minimalist style constantly, or use minimalist techniques as a means to an end. More so than any other 'isms', minimalism has influenced popular music genres which, in turn, have also fed back into minimalism. Listeners who eschew contemporary classical music, might well find themselves enjoying minimalism.

Reich has so far emerged as the leading figure in the movement, having reinvented his own type of minimalism throughout his career. Though the 1960s was an experimental period for him, his first minimalist piece for large instrumental forces did not appear until the *Music for a Large Ensemble* (1978), and his first orchestral piece, *Variations for Winds, Strings and Keyboards* (1979) followed shortly.

Though Reich's works embrace an abundance of music for large ensembles and for voices, purely orchestral works are few and far between, but they include *Three Movements for Orchestra* (1986), and *The Four Sections* (1987). Much of his music for smaller forces, such as the compelling and moving *Different Trains* (1988), plus *Vermont Counterpoint* (1982), *New York Counterpoint* (1985), and *Electric Counterpoint* (1987), are now part of the standard repertoire.

Philip Glass and John Adams are particularly well-known for their operas. Like Reich, Glass's minimalism has transformed itself into something less prescriptive and rigid. But unlike Reich, he has embraced classical genres, by composing ten symphonies (1992–2005), and a number of concertos. Adams has written several orchestral works which are enjoyed by audiences worldwide. These include *The Chairman Dances* from his opera *Nixon in China* (1987), the 1983 string orchestra version of *Shaker Loops* (1978), and two pieces which often accompany each other on concert programs, *Tromba Lontana* (1985), and *Short Ride in a Fast Machine* (1986). With their adherence to recognized tonality, memorable melodic ideas, and the often jazz-inspired use of rhythm, it would seem that these orchestral works, though not minimalist in the 1960s and 1970s sense of that word, have, in their own way, become latter-day classics.

The American contemporary music scene, as we have seen, is diverse and is broadening and re-inventing itself. This is clear to hear in the works of Torke, or in the way in which the minimalists have adapted their own earlier styles. Indeed, the secret of minimalism's success is its dynamic quality. Outside of the USA, there is a wealth of exciting contemporary orchestral music. In Germany, for example, Wolfgang Rihm (b.1952) has produced an amount of orchestral music which has been performed worldwide. In the UK, some of the composers currently being regularly performed include Scottish born James MacMillan (b.1959), who has written three symphonies, plus other post-Romantic, richly scored, large-scale orchestral works, such as the tone poem *The Confession of Isobel Gowdie* (1990).

The accessible and beautifully crafted music of highly acclaimed composer Judith Weir (b.1954) has engaged with the heritage of English music in her *Bright Cecilia: Variations on a Theme by Purcell* (2002) for orchestra. George Benjamin (b.1960) was brought to public prominence when, only twenty, his orchestral piece *Ringed by the Flat Horizon* (1980) received a Proms premiere. Since then, he has produced a number of orchestral works, noted for their shimmering and masterly orchestration. The music of Mark-Anthony Turnage (b.1960) demonstrates his commitment to a wide range of influences, including jazz, as for example in works such as *Riffs and Refrains* (2003) for clarinet and orchestra, and *Your Rockaby* (1994) for saxophone and orchestra. *Three Screaming Popes* (1989) was the piece which launched his orchestral compositional career, whilst *Momentum* (1991) enjoys popularity as a concert-opener.

The successful career of composer, conductor and pianist Thomas Adès (b.1971) shows no sign of diminishing. His music exhibits an immense amount of careful craftsmanship, and orchestral works include his *Violin Concerto, Concentric Paths* (2005).

There is a profusion of exciting orchestral music being written at the moment. Whether we will still be performing or buying the music of Reich, Torke, Adès – whoever – in twenty or a hundred years' time, is anyone's guess. After all, we talk about Schoenberg or Stockhausen more frequently than we perform their music. However, orchestral music is a dynamic force which has been reinventing itself for around three hundred years. There is no reason why it should not maintain this, as long as composers are willing to engage with it. For certain, orchestral concerts, though a minority sport when compared to watching football or soap-operas, will continue to allow live access to some of the greatest and enriching creations on earth.

SUGGESTED FURTHER READING

Books on Music History

Bennett, Roy. *History of Music*. Cambridge: Cambridge University Press, 1987

Nicholas, Jeremy; Ray, Robin. *The Classic FM Guide to Classical Music*. London: Pavilion Books, 1996

Nicholls, David, ed. *The Cambridge History of American Music*. Cambridge: Cambridge University Press, 1998

Russano Hanning, Barbara. *Concise History of Western Music*. London: Norton, 2006

Sadie, Stanley; John Tyrell, eds. *The New Grove Dictionary of Music and Musicians*. London: Macmillan, 2001

Slonimsky, Nicholas. *Lexicon of Musical Invective: Critical Assaults on Composers Since Beethoven's Time*. New York: Norton, 2000

Struble, John Warthen. *The History of American Classical Music*. London: Robert Hale, 1995

Sullivan, Jack. *New World Symphonies – How American Culture Changed European Music*. London: Yale University Press, 1999

Taruskin, Richard. *The Oxford History of Western Music*. New York: Oxford University Press, 2004

Walker-Hill, Helen. *From Sprituals to Symphonies. African American Women Composers and their Music*. Westpoint: Greenwood Press, 2002

Books about the Orchestra and General Repertoire

Del Mar, Norman. *Anatomy of the Orchestra*. California: University of
California Press, 1992

Holoman, D. Kern. *Evenings with Orchestra: A Norton Companion for
Concertgoers*. London: Norton, 1992

Lawson, Colin. *The Cambridge Companion to the Orchestra*.
Cambridge: Cambridge University Press, 2003

Lee, Douglas. *Masterworks of 20th Century Music: The
Modern Repertoire of the Symphony Orchestra*. London:
Routledge, 2002

Peyser, Joan. *The Orchestra*. New York: Watson-Guptill, 2000

Spitzer, John; Zaslaw, Neal. *The Birth of the Orchestra – History of an
Institution, 1650-1815*. Oxford: Oxford University Press, 2005

Books about the Symphony and the Concerto

Keefe, Simon P. *The Cambridge Companion to the Concerto*.
Cambridge: Cambridge University Press, 2005

Kenyon, Nicholas. *The BBC Proms Guide to the Great Concertos*.
London: Faber and Faber, 2004

Kenyon, Nicholas. *The BBC Proms Guide to the Great Symphonies*.
London: Faber and Faber, 2004

Kerman, Joseph. *Concerto Conversations*. Cambridge, Mass: Harvard
University Press, 2001

Linderman, Stephen D. *The Concerto*. London: Taylor & Francis, 2006

Roeder, Michael Thomas. *A History of the Concerto*. Milwaukee:
Hal Leonard Corporation, 1994

Steinberg, Michael. *The Concerto – A Listener's Guide*. New York: Oxford University Press, 1998

Will, Richard; Newcomb, Anthony; Solie, Ruth A. *The Characteristic Symphony in the Age of Haydn and Beethoven*. Cambridge: Cambridge University Press, 2002

Books on the Baroque Period

Anthony, James R. *French Baroque Music from Beaujoyeuix to Rameau*. Portland: Amadeus Press, 2003

Arnold, Denis, ed. *Italian Baroque Masters: New Grove Composer Biographies*. New York: Norton, 1997

Buelow, George J. *A History of Baroque Music*. Bloomington: Indiana University Press, 2004

Hall, John Walter. *Baroque Music*. New York: Norton, 2005

Hutchings, Arthur. *The Baroque Concerto*. New York: Norton, 1961

Palisca, Calude V. *Baroque Music*. Englewood Cliffs: Prentice Hall, 1968

Sadie, Julie Anne, ed. *Companion to Baroque Music*. London: Dent, 1990

Books on the Classical Period, including Beethoven

Downs, Philip G. *Classical Music. The Era of Haydn, Mozart and Beethoven*. New York: Norton, 1992

Rosen, Charles. *The Classical Style*. New York: Norton, 1998

Rushton, Julian. *Classical Music. A Concise History from Gluck to Beethoven*. London: Thames and Hudson, 1986

Wyn Jones, David. *Music in Eighteenth-Century Austria.* Cambridge: Cambridge University Press, 2006

Zaslaw, Neal. *The Classical Era from the 1740s to the End of the 18th Century.* London: Palgrave Macmillan, 1990

Books on the Romantic Period

Plantinga, Leon. *Romantic Music. A History of Musical Style in Nineteenth-Century Europe.* New York: Norton, 1984

Rosen, Charles. *The Romantic Generation.* Cambridge, Mass: Harvard University Press, 1988

Sadie, Stanley, ed. *The New Grove Russian Masters.* London: Macmillan, 1986

Sadie, Stanley, ed. *The New Grove Early Romantic Masters 1 & 2.* London: Macmillan, 1985

Sadie, Stanley, ed. *The New Grove Late Romantic Masters.* London: Macmillan, 1985

Whittall, Arnold: *Romantic Music. A Concise History from Schubert to Sibelius.* London: Thames and Hudson, 1987

Books on the Twentieth and Twenty-first Centuries

Berio, Luciano. *Remembering the Future (Charles Eliot Norton Lectures).* Harvard: Harvard University Press, 2006

Boulez, Pierre. *Orientations.* London: Faber and Faber, 1986

Childs, Barney; Schwartz, Elliott, eds. *Contemporary Composers on Contemporary Music.* New York: Da Capo Press, 1998

Griffiths, Paul. *Modern Music and After.* Oxford: Oxford University Press, 1996

Hall, Michael. *Leaving Home. A Conducted Tour of Twentieth Century Music.* London: Faber and Faber, 1996

Henze, Hans Werner. *Bohemian Fifths. An Autobiography,* London: Faber and Faber, 1998

Jacobson, Bernard. *A Polish Renaissance.* London: Phaidon, 1986

Kater, Michael H. *Composers of the Nazi Era.* Oxford: Oxford University Press, 2000

Levi, Erik. *Music in the Third Reich.* London: Palgrave Macmillan, 1996

Oliver, Michael, ed. *Settling the Score. A Journey Through the Music of the 20th Century.* London: Faber and Faber, 1999

Potter, Keith. *Four Musical Minimalists.* Cambridge: Cambridge University Press, 2002

Reich, Steve. *Writings on Music 1965–2000.* Oxford: Oxford University Press. 2002

Sadie, Stanley, ed. *The New Grove Second Viennese School.* London: Macmillan, 1983

Samson, Jim. *Music in Transition, A Study of Tonal Expansion. 1900–1920.* London: Dent, 1993

Simms, Bryan R. *Music of the Twentieth Century, Style and Structure.* New York: Schirmer, 1986

Whittall, Arnold. *Musical Composition in the Twentieth-Century.* Oxford: Oxford University Press, 1999

Index

A

Adams, John 228, 229; *Chairman Dances (from Nixon in China)* 229; *Short Ride in a Fast Machine* 230; *Tromba Lontana* 230
Adès, Thomas 231; *Violin Concerto, Concentric Paths* 231
Aeolian Hall, New York 189
Aix-la-Chapelle, Peace of 28
Albéniz, Isaac 159
Allgemeine Musikalische Zeitung 34
Alwyn, William 162
Amsterdam (Holland) 25
Anderson, Leroy 206; *Sleigh Ride* 207; *Typewriter* 207
Andriessen, Louis 222; *De snelheid* 222; *Vermeer Pictures* 222
Anhalt-Cöthen, Prince Leopold of 25
Antheil, George 205; *Ballet mécanique* 205
Arabian Nights 92
Arbeau, Thoinot; *Orchésographie* 162
Arnold, Malcolm 161; *Beckus the Dandipratt* 161; *English Dances* 161; *Guitar Concerto* 161; *Symphonies* 161; *Tam O'Shanter Overture* 161
Auden, W. H. 201; *Age of Anxiety* 201
Auld Lang Syne 112
Auric, Georges 175
Auschwitz (Poland) 166

B

Babbitt, Milton 205, 206; *Correspondences* 206; *Relata I & II* 206
Babi Yar (Ukraine) 187
Bach, C.P.E. 36
Bach, J.S. 14, 17, 21, 23, 25, 27, 36, 65, 74, 95, 98, 101, 137, 148, 160, 176, 182; *Air on the G String (from Suite in D)* 27; *Badinerie (from Suite in B minor)* 27; *Brandenburg Concerti* 17, 21, 25, 26, 27, 29; *Cantata No. 150* 76; *Concerto for Two Violins in D minor* 27; *Es ist genug (chorale)* 141; *Harpsichord Concerto in D Minor* 27; *Orchestral Suites* 27; *Overtures* 27; *St. Matthew Passion* 77; *Violin Concertos* 27
Balakirev, Mily 91; *Islamay* 91
Ballets Russes 104, 106, 108, 116, 146, 147, 159, 174
Barber, Samuel 192, 198, 199; *Adagio for Strings* 198; *Capricorn Concerto* 199; *Cello Concerto* 199; *Essays for Orchestra* 199; *Piano Concerto* 199; *School for Scandal Overture* 198, 199; *String Quartet* 198; *Symphony No. 2* 199; *Violin Concerto* 170, 199
Bartók, Béla 15, 22, 83, 96, 102, 123, 129, 140, 145, 150, 151,

243

K

Kabalevsky, Dmitri 179
Kagel, Mauricio 209
Kalevala 126
Khachaturian, Aram 179;
    Gayane 179; *Sparatacus* 179
Kiev (Ukraine) 187
King, Martin Luther 171
Kodály, Zoltán 150, 152, 164;
    Dances from Galánta 152;
    Háry János Suite 152; *Peacock
    Variations* 152
Korda, Alexander; *Things to
    Come* 161
Korngold, Erich 192
Krenek, Ernst 157; *Jonny Spielt
    Auf* 157; *Symphonies* 157
Kubrick, Stanley; *2001: A Space
    Odyssey* 123, 217

L

Lalo, Edouard 100; *Symphonie
    Espagnol* 100
Lambert, Constant 162; *Music
    Ho!* 162; *Rio Grande* 162
Lanner, Josef 95
La Sainte Trinité (Paris) 178
Léhar, Franz 95
Leipzig (Germany) 18, 96
Leipzig Gewandhaus 18
Lenau, Nikolaus; *Don Juan* 123
Les Six 175, 176, 204
Liadov, Anatol 93
Ligeti, György 214, 217,
    218; *Apparitions* 218;
    Atmosphères 217; *Hamburg
    Concerto* 218

Lilburn, Douglas; *Symphony
    No. 2* 167
Linz (Austria) 72
Liszt, Franz 50, 65, 66, 67, 69,
    73, 79, 97, 122, 132, 150, 189,
    190; *Dante Symphony* 66;
    Faust Symphony 66, 67; *Les
    Préludes* 66; *Mazeppa* 66;
    Piano Concerto No. 1 67; *Piano
    Concerto No. 2* 67
Lloyd, George 162
London (England) 18, 28, 32, 33,
    104
Longfellow, Henry Wadsworth;
    Longfellow Hiawatha 89
Lotz, Theodor 38
Lutosławski, Witold 22, 132, 214,
    215, 216; *Cello Concerto* 216;
    Chain 3 216; *Concerto for
    Orchestra* 215; *Double
    Concerto* 216; *Funeral
    Music* 215; *Jeux Vénitiens* 215;
    Livre pour orchestre 216; *Mi-
    Parti* 216; *Piano Concerto* 216;
    Symphony No. 4 216; *Variations
    on a Theme by Paganini* 216

M

MacCunn, Hamish 113; *Land of
    the Mountain and the Flood
    Overture* 113
MacDowell, Edward 188
MacMillan, James 213, 230;
    *Confessions of Isobel
    Gowdie* 230; *Symphonies* 230
Maderna, Bruno 209
Maeterlinck, Maurice; *Pelléas et
    Mélisande* 100

245

Made in the USA
Charleston, SC
19 March 2010